Adorno, Modernism and Mass Culture

Max Paddison

Adorno, Modernism and Mass Culture

Essays on Critical Theory and Music

KAHN & AVERILL, LONDON

First published in 1996 by
Kahn & Averill
9 Harrington Road, London SW7 3ES

Copyright © 1996 by Max Paddison

British Library Cataloguing in Publication Data

A catalogue record for this book is available from the British Library

ISBN 1 871082 61 7

Typeset by Boldface Typesetters, London EC1
Printed in Great Britain by
Redwood Books, Trowbridge, Wilts

Contents

Acknowledgments

I am particularly indebted to my publisher, Morris Kahn, who has waited patiently for this book for more years than I care to mention. His kind encouragement of my work on Adorno and Critical Theory has been greatly appreciated.

Parts of this book have previously appeared in print in various journals. Other parts have been aired initially as conference papers or lectures. Permission from the editors of *Music Analysis and Popular Music* to use previously published material is gratefully acknowledged. Other sources are referenced in the usual way.

I should also like to thank Kevin Thompson, Principal, John Hall, Vice Principal, and Melinda Drowley, Director of Studies of Dartington College of Arts for their generosity in granting me research funds and arranging sufficient space in my lecturing programme to enable me to complete the writing. I am likewise grateful to my academic colleagues at the College for their support, and to many students over the years for their interest.

Between the completion of this book and its appearance I left Dartington to take up an appointment in the Music Department of the University of Durham. I am grateful to my colleagues at

ACKNOWLEDGMENTS

Durham for their consideration in enabling me to find the time to see the book through press.

Among many others who have helped in diverse ways over a lengthy period I should like to thank Jim Samson, Thomas Müller, David Clarke, Graham Green, Rosemary Burn and Peter Siebenhühner. Responsibility for content is, of course, entirely my own.

I dedicate this book with love and gratitude to my partner Linda Marks and to our children Joseph and Olivia.

Max Paddison
Durham
January 1996

Adorno, Modernism and Mass Culture

Introduction

This book has a double aim: to discuss the idea of a critical theory of music, and to do so through considering aspects of Adorno's thinking on modernism and mass culture. Those who have perhaps a passing acquaintance with the ideas of T.W. Adorno might easily assume that his approach, with its high mandarin style and taxing philosophical-sociological apparatus, represents a one-off intrusion of apparently non-musical concerns into the otherwise self-contained world of music and scholarly inquiry. Such assumptions are misleading, however. The context of music, and the ways in which that context – social, cultural, economic, historical – is embedded in the nuts and bolts of music, is itself becoming a central issue, as is apparent from the accelerating academic interest in such areas as popular music studies and what has come to be called critical musicology. Nevertheless, while Adorno is an important figure, he also tends to be seen more generally as simply synonymous with 'critical theory' in music, and this is not always helpful. What is distinctive about his approach can easily remain murky because the conceptual framework is still unfamiliar and is not readily available for useful critical discussion. It is my contention in this book that, while usually seen as identical – and for understandable reasons – Critical Theory and Adorno's particular version of it can also do with prising apart a little, in order to shed some light on the underlying terms of reference in relation to music.

In revising and rethinking material written at various stages over a period of fifteen years, I have tried not to assume a great deal of prior knowledge on the reader's part, although I have resisted as far as possible the temptation to oversimplify. Nevertheless, however one looks at it, the subject matter of Critical Theory is complex and problematic, and the approach can never be other than challenging. The individual essays focus on a limited number of theoretical issues, and the book does not set out to be an extended and detailed exploration. At the same time, given the essays have grown out of a long-term project on Adorno's aesthetic theory and his writings on music, they are, in a very real sense, chips off that block. They are essays in the old sense of trying out ideas, as sketches. In the main they offer different emphases to my earlier study, Adorno's *Aesthetics of Music* (Cambridge, 1993), while also, I hope, complementing it.

I

Some introductory comments on Adorno and Critical Theory are in order here. Philosopher, sociologist and social psychologist who made seminal contributions to aesthetics and cultural criticism, Theodor W. Adorno (1903-69) has to be regarded, perhaps above all else, as one of the most important and penetrating writers on music to come out of the twentieth century. His work resists easy categorization. An inveterate transgressor of traditional discipline boundaries, he brought new critical perspectives from the outside to bear on music and its context, while at the same time being deeply versed in the inner technical aspects of musical practice. A composition pupil of Alban Berg and closely associated with the Second Viennese School composers, he had studied piano with

Eduard Steuermann (the pianist who had given first performances of many important twentieth-century works) and had for a time been editor of the Viennese music journals *Anbruch* and *Pult und Taktstock*. The range of his musical activities is striking. In the late 1920s and early 1930s, for example, he had participated in public debates with the composer Ernst Krenek on free atonality and serialism, and on problems of form, genre and material in the music of the early twentieth century. At the same time he was also engaged in developing a theory of musical performance with the violinist Rudolph Kolisch. In the period of his exile in the United States in the late 1930s and the 1940s he had worked with the sociologist Paul Lazarsfeld on a theory of radio music, collaborated with Hanns Eisler on a project on film music, and made a key contribution to the musical sections of Thomas Mann's novel *Doktor Faustus*. And back in post-war Germany during the 1950s and 1960s, Adorno significantly influenced the debates surrounding the New Music and the avant garde through, for example, his contributions to the Darmstadt Summer School – with all the implications this had, directly or indirectly, for the music of Stockhausen, Boulez, Ligeti and Cage.

A product both of the German tradition of Idealist philosophy and of the artistic experimentation of the Weimar years, Adorno was uniquely placed to act as the theorist of musical modernism. At the same time, as a close observer of the rapid technification of society and the industrialization of culture in the new age of mass media, reinforced by his impressions of American life during his period of exile from Nazi Germany in the late 1930s and the 1940s, he developed an influential theory of mass culture drawing on Marx, Freud and Max Weber, which formed the other pole, dialectically speaking, of his theory of aesthetic modernism. And caught up, like all of his generation, in the rise of Fascism and Stalinism, he was acutely aware of the involvement of art, in spite of itself, with politics, and conversely, of 'the aestheticization of politics', as his colleague Walter Benjamin had put it,[1] which characterized the Nazification of Germany in the 1930s.

Adorno's theoretical approach – Critical Theory – is diverse in its sources, idiosyncratic in its expression, and highly focused conceptually. It also brings with it undeniable problems. The difficulties are at times overwhelming and not always possible to justify. They include a knotted and dense prose style, strong prejudices, and a speculative philosophical-sociological perspective on music which sometimes gives rise to a suspicion that poetic metaphor is masquerading as scientific method. At the same time it has also become impossible to ignore the significance of Adorno's work and its presence within all the central debates around music and its social context, even though it still remains somewhat marginal to mainstream musicology. What he presents us with is a dialectical form of thinking about music which operates through contradiction and through taking ideas to their extremes. As he puts it in that most cryptic of his books, *Minima Moralia*: 'the dialectic advances by way of extremes, driving thoughts with the utmost consequentiality to the point where they turn back on themselves, instead of qualifying them'.[2] It is an approach which itself demands critique and commentary.

II

If anything approaching an introduction to Adorno's music theory is suggested in the course of these essays, it is necessarily a partial and fragmented account, emphasizing particular aspects which seem to me to be of especial importance to the understanding of his work. For the reader motivated to go deeper as well as gain a

[1] Walter Benjamin, 'The Work of Art in the Age of Mechanical Reproduction', *Illuminations*, ed. Hannah Arendt, trans. Harry Zohn (London: Fontana/Collins, 1973), pp.243-4.

[2] Adorno, *Minima Moralia* (1951), trans. E.F.N. Jephcott (London: NLB, 1974), p.86.

sense of the larger picture, some gaps can be filled by turning to a number of available sources. As well as my own earlier study, *Adorno's Aesthetics of Music* (Cambridge: Cambridge University Press, 1993), there is Martin Jay's *Adorno* (London: Fontana, 1984) and his *The Dialectical Imagination* (London: Heinemann, 1973), Susan Buck-Morss's *The Origin of Negative Dialectics* (Sussex: Harvester, 1977), Gillian Rose's *The Melancholy Science* (London: Macmillan, 1978), Lambert Zuidervaart's *Adorno's Aesthetic Theory* (Cambridge, Mass. & London: MIT Press, 1991), and Rose Rosengard Subotnik's *Developing Variations: Style and Ideology in Western Music* (Minneapolis & Oxford: University of Minnesota Press, 1991).

Adorno's work provides the obvious occasion for discussion of the idea of a critical theory of music. A few cautionary words need to be said regarding this, however. My focus here is to some extent a rather modest and limited one, in that by 'Critical Theory' (with significant initial capitals)[3] I mean specifically the approaches initially put forward by the Frankfurt School of Critical Theorists – in particular Horkheimer, Marcuse, Lowenthal, Benjamin, Adorno; then 'second generation' Critical Theorists like Habermas, Schmidt and Wellmer, together with subsequent theorists whose approach has developed from a critique of the work, in particular, of Adorno (for example, Peter Bürger and Konrad Boehmer in Germany, and Susan McClary and Rose Rosengard Subotnik in the USA). While I recognize the importance of the increasing body of work within British and American musicology which certainly falls within a broader notion of critical or cultural musicology – I have in mind, among others, Lawrence Kramer, Caroline Abbate, Jann Pasler, Nicholas Cook, Richard Middleton, John Shepherd and Lydia Goehr – my underlying purpose here is to bring to the fore features of an essentially German theoretical

---

[3] In this book I use initial capitals to indicate specifically the Critical Theory of the Frankfurt School. Without initial capitals, the term 'critical theory' refers to a broader usage.

approach which has as yet, I would argue, had an incomplete reception by Anglo-American musicology. The engagement with French structuralist and post-structuralist theory which characterized the late 1970s and the 1980s, and which was fuelled by availability of translations, somewhat eclipsed the work of Adorno and German Critical Theory (considerably hampered – with the possible exception of certain influential texts by Walter Benjamin – by a shortage of good translations). The engagement with Adorno and Critical Theory is now underway in music, and this book is intended as a contribution to the ensuing debates.

III

The opening essay, 'Critical Theory and Music', considers the defining characteristics of Critical Theory of the Frankfurt variety, and sets out to distinguish it from other forms of theory. It asks the question: what is a specifically critical theory of music?, and offers a broad reading of music history from the perspective of Critical Theory and, in particular, Adorno. This essay has not been published before, but is made up of material from conference papers given between 1990-95. In it I put forward a typology of modes of theorizing music within which to situate the idea of a specifically critical theory of music. I also give an account of the cultural theory and philosophy of history which underpins Critical Theory, and discuss how this leads to a particular interpretation of both aesthetic modernism and of mass culture in terms of the historical exteriorization of subjectivity (what Critical Theorists have called 'the objectification of the Subject') in musical material.

The second essay, 'Adorno's Aesthetics of Modernism', takes the form of a commentary on themes in Adorno's unfinished *Aesthetic Theory*, and discusses how the book addresses the problems of aesthetic modernism. This essay is a revised version of an extended review article published originally in *Music Analysis* in 1987,[4] an article which also served as the sketch which provided the structure for my 1993 full–length study. It is included here, in more concise form and together with some later thoughts, because it also provides a necessary part of the theoretical context for this book. Its reappearance here gives me the opportunity to clear up a possible misunderstanding: that this approach simply summarizes Adorno, pointing to what is already there and plain for all to see in the original. What I have proposed as an interpretation of Adorno's aesthetics, particularly in the 'theoretical model' offered at the end of the essay, does not, of course, occur in this form in the original. Adorno's writing, as is well known, has an inbuilt resistance to summary – indeed, a resistance to 'theory' in any traditional sense. One cannot cream off the content, separated from the extreme concentration of its original formulation. This model is not intended as a précis of Adorno; it is one reading in the light of a particular constellation of related concepts. To change the metaphors, I am using the model as a sketch map for conceptual orienteering, and specifically for homing in on the elusive concepts of 'truth content' and 'authenticity'. As a tool it is perhaps crude, as all models and maps are, being in essence reductive. Nevertheless, I would argue that it has its uses, to the extent that we need to use maps for orientation in unfamiliar terrain. And as a map it is also dispensable, in that, if it assists in giving a sense of location it will have served its purpose. Maps should not be confused, of course, with the terrain itself – they simply plot a limited but significant number of its geographical features, leaving us free to find our own routes through a territory while pointing to some possible destinations. In this, the model put forward here functions as a kind of hitch-hiker's guide to Adorno's aesthetics. But there is obviously no substitute for

[4] Previous versions of this model appeared in (a) the original of this chapter, 'Adorno's *Aesthetic Theory*', *Music Analysis* Vol. 6, No. 3 (October 1987), pp.355–377; and (b) *Adorno's Aesthetics of Music*, pp.59–64.

reading Adorno himself, and these essays are intended to invite the reader to do just that.

The third essay, 'Adorno, Popular Music and Mass Culture', gives a critical reading which attempts to salvage something from a most problematical area in Adorno's work on music. His critique of mass culture has understandably attracted controversy on the grounds that it is élitist and uninformed in its judgments on popular music. At the same time, it is also striking how Adorno's work has become part of the bedrock of contemporary studies on mass culture, to the extent that it has become obligatory to engage with his critique of popular music while simultaneously dismissing the values of bourgeois art music on which that critique is based. What I have done here is to consider Adorno's critique of popular music and mass culture in relation to his critique of the predicament of modern music, underlying which is the now unfashionable notion of 'authenticity' (in the philosophical rather than the early music sense). I ask a question that Adorno himself would have found it difficult to regard as valid: what could constitute an 'authentic' popular music seen within the terms of reference of his claims for an authentic modern music? This essay is a revised version of an article which appeared originally in the journal *Popular Music* in 1982.[5]

The final essay, 'Critical Reflections on Adorno', has not been published before, although parts of it have been given as conference papers and a first version – since substantially revised – was originally written in 1980. It considers some key criticisms that have been levelled against Adorno's work on music. These range from complaints about the density of his prose and his almost exclusive focus on the music of the bourgeois European art music tradition, to attempts to dismiss his entire critical project as having historical relevance only as an expressionistic protest against

[4] Max Paddison, 'The critique criticized: Adorno and popular music', in *Popular Music 2: Theory and Method*, edited by Richard Middleton and David Horn (Cambridge: Cambridge University Press, 1982), pp.201-18.

the rise of Fascism in the 1920s and 1930s, traumatized by the cultural descent into barbarism which led to Auschwitz. I have argued that, with all its limitations and blind spots, Adorno's Critical Theory retains its historical and theoretical relevance, and continues to demand an appropriate level of critical engagement and debate from within the sphere of music.

1 Critical Theory and Music[1]

When Adorno commented in 1962 that 'if so many ... see the thing itself in the actual notes alone, this is not due to the music but to a neutralized consciousness',[2] he was referring to two things: the general conception of music as something entirely transcending the world of everyday reality, and the hermetic character of academic musicology as a discipline. Music as a practice and the ways in which we discuss and theorize it are historically tightly yoked together. It is no coincidence that the historical moment when music begins to develop independently of any direct social function – that is, becomes apparently 'autonomous' – is also the moment when an independent mode of theorizing about music that is later to become musicology in its several varieties first clearly emerges. This moment can be located somewhere around the early to mid-eighteenth century, which saw the rise to

[1] Shorter versions of sections of this essay were given as papers at the University of Surrey in December 1994, and at the Royal Musical Association Conference, 'The Avant Garde and Modernism', King's College, University of London, in February 1990.

[2] T.W. Adorno, *Introduction to the Sociology of Music* (1962), trans. E.B. Ashton (New York: Seabury Press, 1976), p.62.

dominance of autonomous instrumental music and also the appearance of theoretical and philosophical works on music resulting from the rationalizing impulse of the Enlightenment – Rameau's *Traité de l'harmonie réduite à ses principes naturels* (1722) and Rousseau's entries for the *Dictionnaire de musique* (1767) are well known examples. It is, however, in the early nineteenth century in Germany that the autonomy doctrine really comes into its own in music, together with its legitimation by means of a corresponding musical and aesthetic theory.[3] Interestingly, this coincides with two apparently conflicting tendencies at this period: one is the cult of 'inwardness' [*Innerlichkeit*], characterized by a rejection of the world of everyday reality for a heightened experience of the inner world which finds its paradigm in the autonomous musical work; and the other is the increasing commodification of the autonomous work, both as score and as performance, and its need to survive on the open market. These divergent tendencies within nineteenth-century musical life have proved tenacious, and in their lengthy afterlife in the twentieth century have remained firmly fenced off from each other in our collective musical consciousness. The contradiction has not, at least until recently, been well served by a critical analysis within musicology. It is from within this context that Adorno argued: 'The musical experience has been insulated from the experience of the reality in which it finds itself – however polemically – and to which it responds'.[4]

Implied in Adorno's complaint is the need for a particular mode of thinking about music which is able to consider apparently autonomous musical works simultaneously in relation to their context; a form of music theory which is critical and dialectical as

[3] For an interesting account of this process, see Ian Biddle, 'Autonomy, Ontology and the Ideal: Music Theory and Philosophical Aesthetics in Early Nineteenth-Century German Thought' (PhD. Diss., University of Newcastle-upon-Tyne, 1995).

[4] T.W. Adorno, *Introduction to the Sociology of Music*, p.62.

well as historical or analytical. But in spite of – or perhaps because of – its associations with Adorno's name, the idea of a 'critical theory' is still by no means a self evident one in the context of music and musicology. The terms 'criticism' and 'theory' are already spoken for, and in neither case do they correspond to what would be understood by critical theory in philosophy or the social sciences. Adorno's writings on music are frequently misunderstood because his critical sociological aesthetics needs to be placed within a larger theoretical context which embraces philosophy and the social sciences – in particular seen from the perspective of the Critical Theory of the Frankfurt School. Furthermore, the idea of a critical theory needs to be identified more clearly in relation to other modes of thinking about music. Finally, a broad sense of the primary concerns of Critical Theory's philosophy of history is called for in relation to an understanding of what Andreas Huyssen has called 'the Great Divide' – that is, the split between high art (specifically modernism) and mass culture.

1. The Idea of a Critical Theory

As an approach, what has come to be called 'Critical Theory' is particularly associated with the interdisciplinary work of the Frankfurt School and the Institut für Sozialforschung (Institute for Social Research), dating from Weimar Germany in the 1920s and early 1930s.[5] Its key representatives were Max Horkheimer, Herbert Marcuse, Erich Fromm, Leo Lowenthal, T.W. Adorno and, by association, Walter Benjamin. The theoretical foundations are wide-ranging, and go back in particular to Kant, Hegel, and the earlier, Hegelian writings of Marx. Equally important to an understanding of Critical Theory, however, are its origins in Nietzsche, Freudian psychoanalytical theory, the sociology of

---

[5] See Martin Jay, The *Dialectical Imagination: A History of the Frankfurt School and the Institute of Social Research* 1923-50 (London: Heinemann, 1973) for the definitive history.

Max Weber, and in the work of Georg Lukács and Ernst Bloch up to the early 1920s. The post-war years saw the emergence of a second generation of Frankfurt School Critical Theorists, the most significant among whom are Alfred Schmidt, Albrecht Wellmer and, in particular, Jürgen Habermas.

From the start (the Institute for Social Research was founded in Frankfurt in 1923), members of the Frankfurt School shared a common set of research interests. Jürgen Habermas later identified these as concerning forms of socialization, mass media and mass culture, theory of art, and the critique of positivism and science.[6] Indeed, the key theme, which Habermas has called 'rationalization as reification',[7] was the self destruction of reason. Members of the Frankfurt School – in particular Adorno and Horkheimer in their work from the 1940s onwards – argued that the process of rationalization, which since the eighteenth century had appeared to offer the possibility of total enlightenment and emancipation from false forms of thinking through science and the control of nature, had turned against itself. Reason, in what had become its dominant positivist forms as empiricism and pragmatism, had ceased to be self-reflective and critical. They argued for a detailed and sustained critique of the dominant modes of reason which had shaped the world of late capitalism.[8] It was to this project they gave the name 'Critical Theory'.

In brief, Critical Theory has to do with how a theory relates to its object, and how it deals with the contradictions of its object. At the same time it has to do with the contextualization of the object of inquiry – a process which embraces not only the 'objective'

[6] See Jürgen Habermas, 'The Tasks of a Critical Theory of Society', in *Critical Theory and Society*, eds. Stephen Eric Bronner and Douglas MacKay Kellner (London & New York: Routledge, 1989), p.292.

[7] The German term, of which 'reification' is the usual translation, is *Verdinglichung* – to turn an idea into a thing, to petrify it, and render it no longer accessible to critical reflection.

[8] See T.W. Adorno and Max Horkheimer, *Dialectic of Enlightenment* (1947), trans. John Cumming (New York: Herder & Herder, 1972).

14

social and historical context, but also the interaction between individual and society (the 'Subject-Object relationship') which is embedded in that context. In these respects Critical Theory is to be distinguished from what are sometimes called 'objectifying', positivist theories, whether empirical or structuralist in orientation. To the extent that it examines history and historical artifacts as the intertwining of subjectivity and objectivity, the kind of approach represented by Critical Theory offers valuable insights for the contemplation of music – and, indeed, for thinking about musicology itself as a discipline. Before pursuing the particular question as to what constitutes a specifically critical theory of music, however, we need first to address the more general question: what constitutes a critical theory?

In a key article published in 1937 Max Horkheimer made an important distinction between what he called 'traditional' and 'critical' theories.[9] In brief, 'traditional' theories are normally careful to separate themselves from the object of inquiry, and do not usually take themselves also as an aspect of the investigation. 'Critical' theories, on the other hand, claim to be dialectical and self-reflective, in that they take themselves simultaneously in relation to their object. Herbert Marcuse, in an equally seminal essay from the same year, stated that: 'Critical theory is, last but not least, critical of itself and of the social forces that make up its own basis'.[10] Peter Bürger, whose own work has drawn heavily on the Frankfurt School, argues that critical (or what he calls 'dialectical') theories embrace contradiction methodologically, and do not remain external to it, as simply an aspect of their object domain. He writes: 'dialectical criticism ... proceeds immanently. It enters into the substance of the theory to be

[9] Republished in Max Horkheimer, *Traditionelle und kritische Theorie* (Frankfurt/Main: Suhrkamp Verlag, 1970).

[10] Herbert Marcuse, 'Philosophy and Critical Theory' (1937), trans. Jeremy J. Shapiro, *Critical Theory and Society*, eds. Stephen Eric Bronner and Douglas MacKay Kellner (London & New York: Routledge, 1989), p.72.

15

criticized and derives decisive stimuli from its gaps and contradictions'.[11]

Through uncovering its 'gaps and contradictions' critical theories seek to test the validity claims of the object of inquiry (as theory or cultural artifact) to be a seamless and consistent totality. As well as being dialectical and self-reflective, critical theories can be characterized by two other features: their claims to *enlightenment*, in that they seek to illuminate contradiction, the blind spots and absences of the the object of investigation; and *emancipation*, in that they seek to free us from false forms of consciousness and from myth. That is to say, they offer a critique of *ideology*, of the relations of power crystallized in objectivizing theories and in cultural artifacts, through situating them in their social and historical contexts. Jürgen Habermas has argued that: 'Critique becomes ideology critique when it attempts to show that the validity of a theory has not been adequately dissociated from the context in which it emerged; that behind the back of the theory there lies hidden an inadmissible mixture of power and validity, and that it still owes its reputation to this'.[12]

Taking Habermas as his main point of reference, Raymond Geuss distinguishes between what he calls 'scientific' (i.e., traditional empirical) theories and critical theories in three main ways: in terms of aims, cognitive structure and modes of confirmation. He points out that:

i. scientific theories are instrumental and aim at 'successful manipulation of the external world', while critical theories aim at 'emancipation and enlightenment', casting light on hidden coercion and freeing us from it;

ii. scientific theories are 'objectifying', enabling one to 'distinguish clearly between the theory and the objects to which the

[11] Peter Bürger, *Theory of the Avant-Garde* (1974), trans. Michael Shaw (Manchester: Manchester University Press, 1984), p.liv.

[12] Jürgen Habermas, *The Philosophical Discourse of Modernity* (1983), trans. Frederick G. Lawrence (Cambridge: Polity Press, 1987), p.116.

16

theory refers', while critical theories are 'reflective', and make us aware that they are both part of the object-domain they describe and are in part about themselves (that is, they contextualize themselves and give some account of their own genesis);

iii. scientific theories 'require empirical confirmation through observation and experiment', while critical theories must demonstrate that they are 'reflectively acceptable'.[13]

In a nutshell, Geuss defines a critical theory as 'a reflective theory which gives agents a kind of knowledge inherently productive of enlightenment and emancipation'.[14] That is to say, a critical theory, whatever other elements it might have (which do not preclude drawing on empirical or structuralist approaches), will seek to reveal the ideological undercarriage both of itself and of its object domain. Furthermore, critical theories, unlike scientific theories, do not claim to be value-neutral: indeed, as Geuss puts it, a critical theory 'claims to inform [agents] about what interests it is rational for them to have'.[15]

Finally, critical theories tend to have, in a very particular sense, a strongly utopian dimension. This is a utopia against the odds, however, in that the 'facts' of social reality contrast brutally with any utopian vision and may be seen to reduce it to mere fantasy, wishful thinking. But this is, of course, precisely the point: critical theories seek just those moments within the social and cultural totality, within 'the whole way of life' of a culture, which indicate an ideal set of relationships only present in existing social reality as a potential, as a kind of yearning 'for that which is not yet'. Music, particularly in the nineteenth century, became an especially potent repository of such unrealized and socially unrealizable yearnings. The 'promise of happiness' posited by both high art and by mass culture in their different

[13] Raymond Geuss, *The Idea of a Critical Theory: Habermas & the Frankfurt School* (Cambridge: Cambridge University Press, 1981), pp.55-6.

[14] Ibid., p.2.

[15] Ibid., p.58.

ways is seen by Critical Theory as a criticism of social reality as it is.

Taking the range of interests of the Frankfurt School, two are of special relevance to a critical theory of music: *theory of art* (particularly as the aesthetics of modernism), and *theory of mass culture* (or, to use the term favoured by Adorno, the 'culture industry'). The problematic character of a critical theory of music can be seen as inseparable from these two apparently divergent areas of inquiry. On the one hand, aesthetic modernism, like Critical Theory itself, was occupied with the relentless drive towards self-reflection, the questioning of handed-down conventions, the engagement with fragmentation and loss of meaning, the revelation of contradictions, and the search for 'the New'. On the other hand, mass culture can be seen in two distinctly different ways. It can be understood either as the excluded other, that which, in the absence of 'self-reflection', becomes mere material for manipulation of consciousness by the culture industry. Or it can be seen as representing a democratization of culture, the effects of developments in technology and communication being not to constrain and manipulate consciousness, but to release creativity through the enormous increase in access to the technical means of production and distribution. Both of these interpretations of mass culture find a place within the Critical Theory of the Frankfurt School, the first position being represented by Adorno, the second by Walter Benjamin. It is in this larger context that a critical theory of music needs to be understood.

2. Critical Theory and Music: a Typology

In the special context of music not only does the idea of a 'critical theory' have little currency, but the term 'theory' itself has particularly confusing associations. The various senses in which the word 'theory' is used need to be disentangled before we go any further. We need to identify how the term may be understood in relation to a specifically critical theory of music. General usage of the term 'theory' ranges from being simply another word for the 'rudiments of music' and the 'rules of harmony' to, for example, at the other extreme, pitch-class set theory in the analysis of atonal music. On the one hand, it is safe to say that 'theory' tends to be understood somewhat monolithically in relation – or more usually in opposition – to 'practice', either as a set of rules or principles for some aspect of practice or as the body of knowledge that justifies or legitimizes the practice. On the other hand, specifically in relation to musicology (a discipline often regarded by practising musicians as representing all the evils of theory without practice), the term has come to designate an area of inquiry concerned with what could be regarded as the fundamental structuring principles underlying music, as opposed to the specific concerns of analysis, aesthetics, historical musicology or ethnomusicology. And overall, in relation to music the term 'theory' is overwhelmingly associated with empirical, positivist approaches to its subject matter and, when not this, with various forms of structuralism dedicated to the uncovering of technical and formal aspects of the musical work. Seldom indeed is it associated with critique and reflection – beyond, that is, the journalistic practice of criticism and review.

The derivation of the word 'theory' is from the Greek *theorein*, *theoria*, meaning 'contemplation', 'speculation', and having the same roots as the word 'theatre', as 'spectacle', something seen.[16] Intrinsic to the concept is the idea of standing apart from and seeing something in terms of its connections, as the relationship of parts to whole, and also the idea of 'reflection upon', in the sense of holding up a mirror to something. The opposition 'theory-practice' is also long-standing, in the sense of theory informing as well as reflecting practice. The word has come specifically to refer to systematically ordered knowledge. Its association with 'critique'

[16] cf. Arthur Nestrovski, 'Music Theory, Saussure, *Theoria*', *In Theory Only* Vol. 10, No. 6, (May 1988) pp.9-10.

is more recent, but even so dates back at least to the eighteenth-century Enlightenment. In relation to music and the arts, I suggest that the term 'theory' needs to be understood as having several different but interconnected meanings, all of which are concerned in various ways with systematic explanation but not necessarily with speculation and critique. For reasons of simplicity I identify these different 'modes' of theory as a typology with three broad categories:

(1) Theory as codification
(2) Theory as legitimation
(3) Theory as critical reflection

I will expand on this typology briefly here to provide a context for the discussion of critical theory and music which follows.

(1) *Theory as codification*. Theory in this mode is prescriptive, even doctrinal, and is therefore concerned largely with the codification of conventions, the establishment of norms,, and the development of technical skills which, at a certain stage, become 'second nature'. Cultural values are internalized and naturalized, and are not usually directly available for critical examination. This is very much a kind of theory-in-practice which manifests itself in terms of 'spontaneity', 'musicality', and 'sense of form'. It is concerned with 'how things are the way they are', as 'natural', with techniques for achieving particular results, and is empirical in its orientation. It is normative and, in order to function effectively in its own sphere, does not need to be conscious of itself and of its terms of reference.

(2) *Theory as legitimation*. Theory in this mode is largely descriptive, and is concerned with offering explanations and justifications for particular traditions of musical practice (or indeed, for whole world views as cosmologies[17]). It often constitutes

---

[17] One could also include here historical attempts to use music as a metaphor for social or cosmological order. I am indebted to Bob Gilmore for this point.

what is called a 'body of knowledge', and often tells the story of why things are the way they are. It has to do with the legitimation and perpetuation of canons. The theoretical assumptions underlying the various sub-disciplines themselves (e.g. history, aesthetics, analysis, anthropology – and, indeed, 'theory' in the specialized sense in which it is normally used in the academic study of music) are not necessarily part of the discussion.

(3) *Theory as critical reflection.* The concern of theory in this sense is to study how meaning is produced and reproduced within a culture, and to see music as part of a larger 'context of meaning', as a series of discourses characterized by discontinuity. Theory in this mode – essentially interdisciplinary and self-reflective – is critical, in that it sets out to reveal underlying assumptions and values as ideology, and to re-contextualize areas of theory and practice otherwise seen as autonomous and 'natural'. Although drawing on approaches which may include philosophy, sociology, psychoanalysis, and linguistics, it also has to be understood as a level of meta-theory in relation to the kinds of approaches which characterize 'mode 2' and the conventions underlying 'mode 1'. Theory of this kind seeks to be aware of its own terms of reference as well as of its object. It contextualizes itself, and situates music (as both practice and theory) within the sign systems, the discourses – what I call here the 'contexts of meaning'[18] – which constitute 'culture'.

What becomes apparent from this typology is that the three modes of theory identified above can be seen to interpenetrate, although they should not be confused and are not interchangeable. In fact, the relationship between them could be defined more precisely as cumulative. 'Mode 2' theory legitimates and describes what 'mode 1' theory codifies and prescribes, providing various

[18] I propose the use of the term 'context of meaning' (borrowed from the German *Sinnzusammenhang*) as a replacement for the overused 'discourse' – a term which has become as reified through automatic application as the assumptions about meaning it was intended to overthrow.

explanatory schemes to set changing practice in the context of some overarching (usually historical and canonical) narrative. 'Mode 3' theory provides critiques of 'mode 2' theory, questioning underlying assumptions and uncovering contradictions and discontinuities at a level of meta-theory, and also of 'mode 1' theory, particularly as it is embodied and encoded in socio-cultural values and attitudes, and materialized within social structures and cultural artifacts. 'Mode 3' theory is critical specifically in the sense that it is ideology critique.

It also becomes clear that theory and practice are not rigidly separated areas of activity but themselves interact at every stage. In fact, the practice of music and the arts is permeated by 'theory' to a remarkable degree – particularly that of 'mode 1', as the prescription and codification of cultural norms, and of 'mode 2', as the description and legitimation of traditional value systems. At the same time, theory has itself to be seen as a practice in its own right – particularly that of 'mode 3' which, as critical reflection, contextualizes and demystifies cultural norms and traditional values. Through its critique of opaque norms and values such theory renders them transparent through seeing them as part of cultural systems of relationships and of structures of power and domination. It is also ideally self-reflective, in the sense of being able to examine and locate its own assumptions, and emancipatory, in the sense of revealing the conditional character of those assumptions and their claim to absolute and universal validity as ideological.

The concerns of a critical theory of music clearly fall into what I have here called 'mode 3' theory. Seen in this light, the theory-practice relationship is not treated in terms of offering prescriptions or norms for practice, nor of offering descriptive or legitimizing accounts. Instead, the concern is to examine assumptions about music through seeing it as one of the ways in which we 'make sense' of the world, and through which meaning is constructed.

22

However, 'meaning' in music is highly problematical, whether one is talking of high art music or of mass culture. Indeed, one of the key characteristics of art works in general is that they are like riddles – they seem to say something, the precise meaning of which remains always concealed, or at least highly ambiguous. Taken in isolation, particularly through technical analysis, musical works become quite opaque as soon as one goes beyond the most elementary level of interpretation. On the other hand, taken simplistically in a forced relation to their immediate context, they are reduced, as Carl Dahlhaus has argued, to being seen as mere historical, social or political documents – 'a fragment of social reality' denied any aesthetic significance.[19] While Dahlhaus was criticizing what he saw as particular excesses in the sociology of music in the 1960s, he does identify the extreme poles which mark out the field of attempts to understand music. Certainly the ideal would be a critical theory which could encompass these extremes, the dual-character of music: as self-contained, self-referential structure and as social fact. I would argue that contained in Adorno's approach, what I have already called his 'critical socio-logical aesthetics', there is just such a dialectical model, working simultaneously on three levels of 'immanent' analysis, sociological critique and philosophical-historical interpretation. Music is con-sidered in its own terms, as autonomous; and at the same time it is considered in relation to what is 'left out' – that is, in terms of its absences. What is sought, through interpretation, is the repressed social content of music understood in the social context of its production, reproduction, distribution and consumption. (I expand on this model in Chapter 2 in relation to the important idea of the 'truth content' of musical works, and also consider some objections to Adorno's approach in Chapter 4.)

A critical theory would consider music particularly in the

[19] Carl Dahlhaus, *Foundations of Music History* (1967), trans. J.B. Robinson (Cambridge: Cambridge University Press, 1983), pp.8-9.

context of the power relations which underlie the relations of musical production, and would make use of the concept of ideology as 'sets of beliefs unconsciously lived out as values'. It would consider music in terms of ways in which our cultural identities are constructed. It would also consider the effects of developments in technology and communication on the practice of the arts – an effect which has had very concrete results historically (for example, in the development of film and photography, recording techniques, but also the invention of movable type and, it should not be forgotten, of musical notation itself – a technology which made possible the whole tradition of Western art music). It would focus on the contradictoriness of music today, both art music and popular musics, and consider it not only in terms of the classic Marxian emphases on class and the economy, but also in terms of race and gender[20] (two areas which the first generation Critical Theorists certainly neglected). Above all, the theoretical models offered by a critical theory would emphasize that, although music and the arts in general may seem – in the West at least – the most individual and personal of activities, they are also always social. In short, music would be considered in terms of its *mediated* – that is, non-immediate, indirect – relationship to that which lies 'outside' it. It is in this sense that cultural artifacts tell us something about the world and the way we relate to it, and it is in this sense, therefore, that art works may be regarded as a form of knowledge. I would understand Edward Said as referring to this kind of approach when he writes in *Musical Elaborations* of the possibility of mapping 'an ensemble of political and social involvements, affiliations, transgressions, none of which is easily

[20] The work of Susan McClary in the area of music, gender and sexuality has drawn tellingly on Adorno and Critical Theory (in combination with Foucault). See especially *Feminine Endings* (Minnesota & Oxford: University of Minnesota Press, 1991).

24

reducible either to simple apartness or to a reflection of coarse reality'.[21]

The task of a critical theory of music would be to illuminate the connections between, to use Valéry's term, the 'closed world' of the musical work and the world outside. These connections, the meaning of the work, are not seen as simple and direct, but as complex and multi-layered. They manifest as contradictions, as gaps and absences, both in formal/structural terms within the work and in the autonomous work's relation to its 'social other'. The surface of the work, its appearance, is seen as a cipher to other levels of meaning, a cipher which must be deciphered before the significance of its patterns can be revealed. It is not, however, a question of a single, fixed meaning hidden behind appearances. The relation is more paradoxical than that. The deciphering, or interpretation is more in the nature of a friction between two extremes which leads to an illumination, in the light of which the poles of the original contradiction disappear. As Adorno describes it: 'Authentic philosophic interpretation does not meet up with a fixed meaning which already lies behind the question, but lights it up suddenly and momentarily, and consumes it at the same time'.[22]

A critical theory of music thus becomes a parallel process to that of the musical work itself. Just as the work of art may be understood as the embodiment of the historical intertwining of subjectivity and objectivity, so would a critical theory of music aim to illuminate and interpret that relationship.

3. Critical Theory and the Enlightenment Project

Fundamental to the idea of Critical Theory in the Frankfurt

[21] Edward Said *Musical Elaborations* (1991) (London: Vintage Books, 1992), p.71.

[22] T.W. Adorno, 'The Actuality of Philosophy', trans. uncredited, *Telos* 31 (1977; orig. German unpubl. 1931), p.127.

School sense is a cultural theory – essentially a philosophy of history – which is both Marxian and Weberian in its origins. It is Marxian insofar as it espouses a conflict theory of historical movement, in terms of changes in the mode of production which characterize a society and the changing balance between the forces and relations of production. It is a distinctly modified Marxism, however, in that it argues that in the period of late capitalism the radical role of the proletariat in the class struggle has been neutralized by the effects of mass culture. The emphasis is firmly on the Marxian concept of the commodity, and, in the version of Marx and Hegel mediated through Georg Lukács, on commodity fetishism and reification. It is Weberian in that it argues that it is rationality – specifically means-ends or instrumental rationality – that pervades Western culture as a whole and which characterizes the development of society in the direction of ever greater technical and bureaucratic efficiency, towards what Adorno had called the 'administered world'. For Weber, the process of rationalization is what constitutes modernity, and he identifies it with the societal process of modernization itself. But while the idea of rationality, as reason, promised freedom and emancipation as viewed from the eighteenth-century Enlightenment, Weber's use of the concept in the early twentieth century has a distinctly negative aspect, in that it dispenses with any sense of utopian promise, emphasizing instead the dominating and enchaining aspects of rationality. Albrecht Wellmer identifies these unreconciled opposites in Weber's concept of rationalization in the following terms, while also pointing to its legacy for Frankfurt School Critical Theory, especially that of Adorno and Horkheimer:

> Weber, in a way, continues the tradition of his nineteenth-century predecessors when he analyses the transition to modernity as a process of rationalization ... However, through his analysis of the institutional correlates of progressive rationalization – capitalist economy, bureaucracy, and professionalized empirical science – he shows at the

same time that the "rationalization" of society does not carry any utopian perspective, but is rather likely to lead to an increasing imprisonment of modern man in dehumanized systems of a new kind – to an increasing "reification", as Weber's disciple Lukács would later on call it. The paradox, that "rationalization" connotes both emancipation and reification at the same time, remains unresolved in Weber's theory; it is this paradox which Adorno and Horkheimer later tried to resolve through their conception of a "dialectic of Enlightenment".[23]

The diagram (p.28) attempts to put into schematic form some of the orientation points which need to be located in order to discuss the 'project of Enlightenment' in Frankfurt School terms. It derives in part from an interpretation of Adorno and Horkheimer in their seminal text, *Dialectic of Enlightenment* (1947). It is not, of course, to be found in that book in this form, and is offered here, with all the generalization and simplification it implies, only as a starting point for more elaborate discussion.

What this diagram seeks to identify are key points of reference for the 'Enlightenment project' and its aftermath. Central to an understanding of the Enlightenment is the concept of rationality, the application of reason to all aspects of society. What this meant historically was, to use a particularly cumbersome term, the demythologization of the world, emancipation from religion and from aristocratic patronage, the rise of empirical scientific method (hallowed traditional beliefs no longer accepted as time-honoured truths, but instead subjected to systematic experiment, the evidence of the senses); a belief in progress towards a better form of society and towards the scientific control of the forces of nature; increased efficiency through the bureaucratic organization of life and the rational organization of the production of goods, their

[23] Albrecht Wellmer, 'Reason, Utopia, and the Dialectic of Enlightenment', in *Habermas and Modernity*, ed. Richard J. Bernstein (Cambridge: Polity Press, 1985), p.41.

CULTURE AS A HISTORICAL PROJECT
Context: 18th-Century European Enlightenment and its consequences

ENLIGHTENMENT
(as progress of rationality towards ever
greater control of 'nature' and towards
emancipation from myth; characterized
by change, development, and the idea
of 'the New'; aspiration towards
autonomy; dynamic)

CULTURE/HISTORY
(as dominant 'spirit of
the age' – e.g., the
rationality principle;
industrialization;
technology; division
of labour; increasing
social fragmentation)

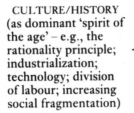

NATURE
(as that which 'simply
is'; raw material'; also
as the 'excluded
other'; as utopian
dream of organic
wholeness)

MYTH
(as 'pre-rational', pre-capitalist attempts
to control nature and make sense of the
world; tradition; harmony with nature;
acceptance of dependence on 'nature',
as 'fate'; mimetic; epic; static)

standardization and mass distribution and marketing to consum-
ers; and the increasing control of the labour process effected by
the division of labour. These developments, which came about
with the rise of the middle classes to political as well as economic
power in Western Europe, also brought with them profound social
changes (this is, of course, the period of the Industrial Revolution
and of the French Revolution). And these social changes – brought
about by fundamental changes in the way in which society

produced, distributed and consumed its goods – affected equally profoundly the ways in which the arts were produced and received.

The polarities identified in the diagram call for some interpretation. In critical theoretical terms they need to be understood as 'mediating each other through their extremes'. That is to say, history/culture defines itself in relation to, or against, 'nature'. At the same time culture also becomes reified, and takes itself as 'natural'. The concept of 'nature' understood in dialectical terms is a particularly mutable one. The idea of 'nature' is, of course, itself historical, in the sense that it is historically and culturally constructed. Historically there has always been a powerful current within Western culture (and within German culture in particular), which has argued either for the 'naturalness' of its own foundations, or, more often perhaps, for the urgent need to return to earlier supposedly natural foundations. This tendency, which in broad terms is associated with nationalism, has obvious political implications. To resort to the 'nature' argument, whether in music or in politics, is to resort to the ultimate, beyond which there can be no further argument – 'these are naturally-ordained laws', 'this is how it is', 'this is how it has always been', 'this is how it should be'. The appeal to 'nature' is the appeal to order, and to philosophical 'first things', to that which is unchanging beyond changing appearances. It can be recognized as an attempt to cope with chaos, disintegration and fragmentation by trying to return to a time when things were considered to be stable, in an idealized and distant, perhaps classical or heroic, pre-industrial, pre-modern past evoking the image of a harmonious community without alienation, with the bonds created by language and rootedness in the soil. It usually involves drawing on myth to replace history, the dynamics of which it wishes to freeze in favour of stasis and repetition. Interestingly, such appeals to nature either ignore the destructive side of nature in the raw or attempt to rationalize this through claiming it is in accord with some notion of evolution, as survival of the fittest, and racial purity. It contrasts markedly with the liberal humanism of what Jürgen Habermas has called 'the Enlightenment Project' – that other important strand in the development of a specifically European consciousness, with its sense of necessary historical change and 'progress' towards the new and unknown, and which is characterized by rational inquiry and the ever-increasing control and manipulation of the material of nature. In both of these extreme cases – the traditionalist with its mythical, irrational and restorative appeal to nature, and the liberal-humanist with its historical, rational, progressivist, modernizing and manipulative view – 'nature' as a concept can only be understood as the reflection of particular historical needs, or as the projection and reading of those needs on the face of nature. Walter Benjamin had argued in *The Origin of German Tragic Drama*, for example, that for the German Baroque drama of the seventeenth century, 'it is fallen nature which bears the imprint of the progression of history'.[24]

As we have seen, Max Weber had used the concept of 'rationalization' to identify what he saw as a process of increasing organization, administration and control of society and the domination of nature through the natural sciences.[25] He also suggested, however, that the effects of this process were to be seen in Western art music, in terms of the rationalization of tuning systems, musical instrument technology, the development of complex notational systems and the complex polyphony that this made possible, the development of the orchestra, and of large-scale instrumental forms.[26] This concept was taken up by both Lukács and Adorno to

[24] Walter Benjamin, *The Origin of German Tragic Drama*, trans. John Osborne, with an introduction by George Steiner (London: NLB, 1977), p.180.

[25] See Max Weber, *The Protestant Ethic and the Spirit of Capitalism* (1904-5), trans. Talcott Parsons (London: George Allen & Unwin, 1930).

[26] See Max Weber, *The Rational and Social Foundations of Music* (1911, 1921), trans. and ed. Don Martindale, Johannes Riedel and Gertrude Neuwirth (Carbondale: Southern Illinois University Press, 1958).

discuss the rationalization of the external world (in terms of the conditions within which art had to function) and the inner rationalization represented by the consistency of the form of the art work. In relation to music the historical process of rationalization, identified by Weber as the domination of Western society by means-ends rationality, is identified by Adorno with the development of music's autonomy. At the same time he also identifies it with the development of mass culture.

4. Autonomy and Social Function

The debate over the autonomy of art in relation to its social function as commodity is central to Critical Theory and to its theory of art (specifically modernism) and of mass culture. The debate was given its clearest form in the exchange of letters and essays between Adorno and Walter Benjamin in the mid-1930s.[27] Indeed, this exchange provides us with one of the most stimulating and instructive examples available of dialectical critique in action. Underpinning it is the Marxian concept of 'commodity fetishism'. The commodity, according to Marx, is the product of human labour, and yet takes on the character of a 'natural' object because the process of human labour which went into its production is concealed in the object itself. It becomes dream-like and 'phantasmagorical',[28] to use Marx's famous term – a fetish object, given mysterious powers over us. And yet this dream-like quality is not directly part of our consciousness: it is itself a product of our alienated relationship to the commodity, a product of our lack of consciousness of the real relations of production concealed within the fetish object. In criticizing what he saw as Benjamin's mystification of the relationship between commodity fetishism and

---

[27] See, for example, Ernst Bloch et al. *Aesthetics and Politics*, ed. Ronald Taylor (London: NLB, 1977), pp.110-141.
[28] Karl Marx, *Capital*, vol.1 (1867), trans. Ben Fowkes (Harmondsworth: Penguin, 1976), p.165.

consciousness in his work on Baudelaire, Adorno had argued that: 'The fetish character of the commodity is not a fact of consciousness; rather, it is dialectical, in the eminent sense that it produces consciousness'.[29]

During the period of the Enlightenment (although in part the outcome of a process that had begun much earlier and could be dated back to the Renaissance), European art music achieved its autonomy status through freeing itself from any immediate social function (for example, in magic, religious ritual, dance, or work). This is particularly striking in the case of music, in that its autonomy coincides with the emergence of a dominant tradition of instrumental music and its corresponding forms emphasizing inner logic and consistency, and a tendency within this tradition towards economy of means and integration of material – something which we have already considered in relation to Max Weber's concept of 'rationalization'. Music, like the other arts, became secularized, and increasingly during this period became one of those modes of art – like literature and the visual arts – through which the individual subjectivity (what Lukács and Adorno would call the 'bourgeois Subject') reflects upon itself and its experience of life at a distance from 'everyday life'. At the same time, this distanced 'self-reflection' is recognized as having a collective content through its materials and techniques (the handed-down genres, formal schemata and stylistic norms) and through the context of its reception (the emerging tradition of middle class public concerts and the continuation of a long-standing tradition of home music-making). Thus, during the eighteenth and early nineteenth centuries in European art music there is a continuity between music's autonomy status and its social function – social function understood here not as immediate practical function, but rather as the ideological function of

---

[29] Theodor Adorno, 'Letters to Walter Benjamin' (1936-8), trans. Harry Zohn, in Ernst Bloch et al., *Aesthetics and Politics*, p.111.

affirming or celebrating the values and aspirations of the rising middle classes. It can be argued that this was not a function of which music itself needed to be conscious.

All this changes after the mid-nineteenth century with the emergence of movements like Symbolism and Aestheticism. This signals the important tendency normally referred to as 'aesthetic modernism', and the appearance of this tendency could be seen to have distinct political and historical origins. That is to say, on the one hand one of the most striking features of aesthetic modernism was the retreat from any sense of social commitment after the failed revolutions of 1848. The disillusion of artists like Baudelaire and Wagner bears witness to this. The historian Eric Hobsbawm has argued that: 'Not until the 1848 revolutions destroyed the romantic hopes of the great rebirth of man, did self-contained aestheticism come into its own.'[30]

On the other hand, it has also to be recognized that the retreat from social commitment and the 'flight into formalism', while undoubtedly the most significant tendency for the development of a distinctively modernist aesthetic, was also accompanied by a variety of notable attempts to restore to art its lost social function – or at very least, to avoid falling into formalist abstraction – through making use of 'everyday' or 'popular' materials. In the later nineteenth century this tendency is represented by the naturalism of writers like Zola, by the realism of painters like Courbet, and the upsurge of nationalism in music. What was more significant than this, however, was the functionalization of culture in another way – something already underway by the late nineteenth century: the effective development of a mass culture geared towards mass consumption and with the function of entertainment, and employing the industrial and technological means of mass production and mass marketing.

[30] Eric Hobsbawm, *The Age of Revolution* 1789-1848 (London: Weidenfeld & Nicholson, 1962; Sphere/Cardinal, 1988), p.325.

In an attempt to identify particular stages in the tendency of art towards autonomy in the West, Peter Bürger has put forward a categorization which considers the arts over three historical periods – the late middle ages (where he characterizes the dominant type of art as 'sacral'), the Baroque period (where he characterizes it as 'courtly') and the 'bourgeois period' (the period from the Enlightenment up to the twentieth century, characterized by the free market).[31] This historical process may also be seen as movement of the historical Subject from collective to individual modes of production and reception, from heteronomy to autonomy. While this is a somewhat reductionist and simplistic scheme, it does serve to provide some useful orientation points.

Viewed historically, argues Bürger, the arts can be seen in relation to:

Church patronage (Sacral Art)
(e.g. the late Middle Ages)

Aristocratic patronage (Courtly Art)
(e.g. the Baroque Period, 17th and early 18th centuries)

Free market (Bourgeois Art)
(from the 'Enlightenment Period' of 18th century to the present day)

In reality, of course, there are many overlaps between these historical categories. For example, the church continues in a sense to patronize music. Aristocratic patronage of the arts coexisted with church patronage for whole historical periods. And examples of 'bourgeois art', even if not perhaps in a 'free market' as understood today, can be found in earlier historical periods. Nevertheless, the thrust of Bürger's model is clear enough when understood within the context of its evident origins within Adorno's Hegelian-Marxian philosophy of history: particular historical (i.e. socio-economic) conditions produce particular forms of art which have a

---

[31] Peter Bürger, *Theory of the Avant-Garde*, pp.47–8.

distinctive (and 'necessary') relation to the *dominant* power relations which characterize a period. The key idea is dominant power relations. This is not to say that other modes of art did not survive within a particular period. What it does say is that all art, as all aspects of culture in the sense of 'whole way of life', has no choice but to be affected and shaped by the dominant relations of power which characterize a society in terms of the way in which that society produces, reproduces, distributes and consumes the goods which define it. Thus, while anachronistic institutions and their artifacts may survive within a very different set of socio-economic conditions to those which originally gave rise to them, they will be peripheral to the new relations of power while at the same time being unable to escape the effects of the new conditions.

Bürger also considers the categories of sacral, courtly and bourgeois art in terms of the *function* of art, how it was produced and how it was received or consumed.[32] What his typology indicates is the historical shift from (1) art as cult object in the service of the church (for example, the use of painting and sculpture to portray biblical stories to a largely illiterate public in the mediaeval period), and where art was produced collectively, as a craft and the mode of reception was institutionalized as collective, to (2) a system of court patronage, where art was used as the self-portrayal of court society, but where the mode of production becomes individual, even though the reception is collective (for celebratory and sociable court purposes). Courtly art he sees as transitional, in a sense, because already art is becoming autonomous, in that 'the artist produces as an individual and develops a consciousness of the uniqueness of his activity',[33] and in that such art is itself in the process of emancipation from ties with religion. With bourgeois art, however, he argues that increasingly during the 'bourgeois period' the production and reception of art are now both

[32] Ibid. p.48.
[33] Ibid. p.47.

individual, and that art is now an activity in which the middle classes seek to understand themselves, to make sense of their world. But, in contrast to art in earlier historical periods, such art now becomes separated from the practice of life, and this 'self-understanding', increasingly contradictory in character, is thrown in upon the inner workings of art works themselves, understood as the 'objectification of the Subject'. Furthermore, the avant garde itself begins to question the whole concept of art, and turns against the institutions of art. At the same time, however (although Bürger does not emphasize this in his model), art works, in becoming individualized and apparently completely autonomous, also lend themselves easily to commodification and simply become assimilated to the leisure and entertainment industry. As Adorno put it in *Aesthetic Theory*: 'Before the French Revolution artists were retainers: today they are entertainers.'[34]

While basing his theory on a critique of those of Lukács and Adorno, Bürger considers that they both 'argue within the institution that is art, and are unable to criticize it as an institution for that very reason. For them, the autonomy doctrine is the horizon within which they think'.[35] Instead, Bürger makes a key distinction between modernism and the avant garde, and emphasizes the avant garde as opposition to the institution of art itself. He argues that the object of attack by the European avant-garde movements (and he clearly has Dadaism and Surrealism in mind here) is not earlier forms and styles of art, but rather the institution and autonomy status of art itself. What is being thrown into question by the avant garde is the way art functions in society – that is, on the one hand as quite separate from the practice of life and, on the other hand, as a commodity in spite of itself.[36]

In Bürger's reading, the avant garde attacks the autonomy

[34] T.W. Adorno, *Aesthetic Theory*, p. 376.
[35] Peter Bürger, *Theory of the Avant-Garde*, p.lii.
[36] Ibid., p.49.

status of high art – and this very much includes aesthetic modernism – and seeks to break down the barriers between art and life. In this repect it is to be distinguished from modernism, although the distinction is not always easy to maintain. As I have suggested, the theory of the avant garde put forward by Bürger is enormously indebted to Lukács and, above all, to Adorno. Indeed, it clearly arose initially from an attempt to explicate Adorno's work. In the process of trying to clarify Adorno's thought through focusing on the concepts of modernism and the avant garde, Bürger inevitably found himself systematizing it. Through identifying and categorizing elements of Adorno's particular variant of Marxian and Weberian theories of history, Bürger doubtless found he had developed theoretical models which had implications beyond the position Adorno himself had argued, for example, in his notion of the 'historical dialectic of musical material'. The influence of Bürger's Adornian trope has been nevertheless to hijack the concept of the 'avant garde', and to limit it to that particular historical strand represented by Dadaism and Surrealism. His explication cum critique of Adorno has undoubted explanatory value, in that it uses the terms 'modernism' and 'avant garde' to make important and useful conceptual distinctions. At the same time, however, it can be argued that these distinctions could equally well be understood as different tendencies within modernism itself: it would be a pity, therefore, if in the process they resulted in the reification of the concept of the avant garde, thus inhibiting the fluidity of its interaction with a much broader notion of modernism.

Whatever one chooses to label these distinctions, it is clear that, even by the turn of the century, art's autonomy status was under threat from a revolution within art itself – the attempt of art to negate itself represented, somewhat quixotically perhaps when viewed in retrospect, by that subversive tendency within modernism Bürger labels the 'avant garde'. But what is also clear, even from this brief consideration, is that historically the autonomy status that art in the West had acquired was already under a far more potent threat from changed social conditions – the conditions of production, distribution and consumption within which it had already come to function well in advance of the modernist period. Seen from the viewpoint of Critical Theory these changing historical and social conditions had thrown up some telling contradictions. The rise to power of the middle classes (in the late eighteenth- and early nineteenth-centuries, it should be pointed out, a radical, even revolutionary class in many parts of Europe and also initially in the United States) brought with it interesting and paradoxical developments in the arts. Strangely, for a society dedicated to the ideal of applied reason, the arts – and in particular music – became one of the last bastions of the 'irrational', or perhaps more accurately 'the not-yet-rationalized', where people could relax from the pressures of an increasingly controlled and bureaucratized work place and gain a kind of profane version of spiritual uplift. At the same time, however, the place music occupied within society was increasingly organized according to the market principles which motivated society as a whole. And, furthermore, the ways in which composers organized their materials in the internal 'formation' of their works also became increasingly rational and controlled through the development of new techniques and the application of technological possibilities originally developed outside the arts (for example, developments in musical instrument technology, in mechanical reproduction, and later in the nineteenth century, with the invention of the technologies of photography and film).

Another paradox was that, as society at large became more industrialized and functionalized, high art music became increasingly separated from any direct social function. (This was also the period when the idealization of nature became a noticeable feature of a progressively industrialized and urbanized culture – a culture which was, at the same time, controlling and exploiting nature, and which had its location in the city.) Art became increasingly autonomous and, especially after the 1850s, retreated into its own world, into what came to be called 'formalism', bolstered by the aesthetic doctrine of 'art for art's sake'. Baudelaire's veneration of Wagner, for instance, and Walter Pater's call for music to become the mode of art to which all others aspire, are key examples of this. This allowed music, and the arts in general in their emulation of music, to become the ultimate fetish object. By the late nineteenth century and early twentieth century this tendency, following the lead of so-called 'absolute' music of the period, reached its extreme in the work of the Symbolist poets, writers and painters. It was an art which rejected the world of everyday reality, constructing in its place an alternative reality, internally consistent and tightly organized, but standing in opposition to the functionality of the real world and the increasing dominance of a mass culture. It was also, in a sense, 'against nature', in that it tended to reflect upon and reveal its own artifice, the thoroughly organized character of its own inner processes.

On one level the split between art and life, as it was called by Valéry, could be seen simply as that between Romantic Idealism and scientific positivism. That is to say, the extreme solipsism of aesthetic modernism could be understood as a rejection of the scientific positivism and moral–utilitarian values of the industrialized late nineteenth century. Thus the split between art's autonomy status and its social function comes nearer to that expressed by Hugo von Hofmannsthal, when he wrote in 1894: 'Today, two things seem to be modern: the analysis of life and the flight from life ... One practises anatomy on the inner life of one's mind, or one dreams'.[37] The rationality of the world of empirical reality, as increasing technical control over material and the domination of nature, enters the closed world of the art work. In the process, however, its character is changed: from means-ends (or instrumental)

[37] cited in James McFarlane, 'The Mind of Modernism', in *Modernism 1890–1930*, eds. Malcolm Bradbury and James McFarlane (Harmondsworth: Penguin, 1976, 1986), p.71.

rationality to what Max Weber had called 'value rationality'. That is to say, the rationality of art is not directed towards the organization, control and manipulation of the external world. Instead, it is geared towards the apparently irrational end of a lack of direct function, a lack of apparent purpose, towards the creation of something which, although it has all the manifestations of being purposeful, 'functional' and consistent within the enclosed world of its form, is useless for all practical purposes.

It is in this radical split between art and life and between modernism and mass culture that, from the perspective of Critical Theory, the dilemma of a so-called 'authentic' art since the mid-nineteenth century can be located. The various arts movements which have characterized the modernist tendency in the twentieth century, whatever their political orientation (and it is an interesting and confusing fact that particular developments in modernism and the avant garde have lent themselves to being claimed by both extremes of the political spectrum), can all be understood as strategies to rationalize this split – either as attempts to restore to art its lost social function (for example Brecht's epic theatre and Eisler's politically engaged musical praxis), or to justify its apparent functionlessness (for example, both Schoenberg's and Stravinsky's continuation of the 'art for art's sake' aesthetic).

5. Postscript: Modernism, Postmodernism, and Mass Culture

Undoubtedly Adorno's work has set the seal on the idea of a critical theory of music, even though in the process much misunderstanding has arisen as to what precisely it is that he has done. I have not seen it as my purpose in this essay to go into the detail of the application of his theories to music, as I have already addressed this at length elsewhere.[38] My concern here has been to consider

[38] See Max Paddison, *Adorno's Aesthetics of Music*.

Critical Theory in broader terms, and to identify its grand themes in relation to its theory of art, before focusing on aspects of Adorno's modernist aesthetic theory and his critique of popular music. Before leaving the grand themes, however, I should like to comment briefly on the development of a particular cluster of these themes *post* the first generation of Frankfurt School theorists. It concerns certain issues in the relationship of modernism and the avant garde to mass culture and postmodernism. It also concerns the 'post-avantgarde', the rejection of modernism, and the attempts in particular of Andreas Huyssen and Jürgen Habermas to understand this phenomenon. The call has been for a new critical paradigm after Adorno.

Andreas Huyssen, for instance, has argued that, while it was quite understandable that Adorno and others (like the American art critic Clement Greenberg) should have insisted on the absolute separation of high art and mass culture because 'the political impulse behind their work was to save the dignity and autonomy of the art work from the totalitarian pressures of fascist mass spectacles, socialist realism, and an ever more degraded mass culture in the West . . . this project has now run its course and is being replaced by a new paradigm, the paradigm of the postmodern.'[39] Huyssen accepts Bürger's distinction between modernism and the avant garde, and suggests that the postmodern was born out of the iconoclastic and adversarial character of the avant garde. In order to be understood adequately, he maintains, both modernism and postmodernism need to be seen in terms of their contrasting relationships to mass culture.[40] In essence, of course, the differences in that relationship could be seen as starkly simple: either a modernist rejection of mass culture and a negation of its commodity-character, or a postmodernist rejection of modernist

---

[39] Andreas Huyssen, *After the Great Divide: Modernism, Mass Culture, Postmodernism* (Bloomington: Indiana University Press, 1986), pp.ix-x.

[40] Ibid., p.viii.

alienation and the embracing of mass culture and affirmation of its commodity character. But the demise of modernism and the avant garde with the collapse of the heroic dream of the perpetually New is in part because the ideal of the autonomous art work is no longer sustainable due to changed social and cultural conditions since the late 1950s. Seen from an Adornian perspective, this must also signal the end of the critical, oppositional and self-reflective work of art and the triumph of mass culture, a culture of total affirmation of the status quo. Huyssen, however, while recognizing the strongly con-servative impulses associated with postmodernism (whether in the desire to restore high art to its pedestal, to embrace mass culture, or even to establish some version of an imagined pre-modern arca-dia), argues that in its sheer diversity a critical postmodernist arts practice should be possible, and indeed is necessary. He sees these critical potentialities as lying in four areas in particular: the chal-lenge to what he calls modernism's culture of 'inner and outer imperialism'; the creative force unleashed by the women's move-ment; the broad critique of modernity and modernization mounted by the ecology movement; and a growing awareness of other, non-Western cultures not based on conquest and domination.[41]

Jürgen Habermas, on the other hand, does not share such optimism regarding postmodernism and its associated tendencies. He argues that, while modernism may have failed, it still remains an incomplete project. Aesthetic modernism is one aspect of the larger culture of modernity and the historical process of modern-ization of which postmodernism also needs to be seen as part. Habermas, in his 'theory of communicative action', differentiates between three cultural spheres (which he derives from Max Weber): science, morality (including law), and art. Since the thorough-going attempt at social rationalization carried out in the eighteenth-century Enlightenment, these three cultural spheres have become the domain of professionals, resulting in the

[41] Ibid., pp.219-20.

development of objective science, universal morality and law, and autonomous art. He suggests that 'the Enlightenment philosophers wanted to utilize this accumulation of specialized culture for the enrichment of everyday life – that is to say, for the rational organization of everyday social life'.[42] The subsequent reification of these spheres, however, has meant that they have become split off, as a culture of expertise, from everyday communication. Attempts to negate this culture of expertise and establish communication with the everyday life-world fail because they operate only within one or other of these cultural spheres and cannot effect real change on the totality. An example of such a failure, he considers, was the attempt of the avant garde with its Dadaist and Surrealist revolts to undermine the institution of art itself and level the boundaries between art and life. Habermas sees the need for 'a differentiated relinking of modern culture with an everyday praxis'.[43] But his suggestions for the realization of such a project are disappointingly unspecific at this stage, and he confesses that 'the chances for this today are not very good'.

Habermas points to the striking contradiction between the ongoing encouragement of capitalist modernization throughout the Western world and and the emergence of conservative intellectual trends which are critical of cultural-aesthetic modernism. He notes the tendency of antimodernist critics to blame the effects of the processes of socio-economic modernization on what they see as the excesses of cultural-aesthetic modernism. The current engagement of Critical Theorists like Habermas with post-modernist/antimodernist critics hinges on a fundamental disagreement regarding the nature of subjectivity and the relation of the Subject to the objective 'life-world'. Critical Theorists oppose to the decentered Subject of postmodernism the persistent

[42] Jürgen Habermas, 'Modernity – An Incomplete Project', in *Postmodern Culture*, ed, Hal Foster (London: Pluto Press, 1985), p.9.
[43] Ibid., p.13.

modernist ideal of an autonomous self-reflecting Subject, battered and fragmented as it has now undoubtedly become. If the history of music is taken as one manifestation of the historical development of subjectivity, then the implications of an analysis of this kind for an understanding of music today in its relation to the socio-economic totality are profound.[44] The roots of such an analysis are to be found deep in Adorno's aesthetic theory.

[44] See Alastair Williams, 'New Music and the Claims of Modernity' (PhD. diss., University of Oxford, 1991) for a fuller account of directions in Critical Theory and music since Adorno, and for an attempt to ground the theoretical approach in the analysis of compositional structures, particularly in the music of Boulez, Cage and Ligeti.

2 Adorno's Aesthetics of Modernism[1]

Adorno's *Aesthetic Theory*, his last and in some ways most ambitious book, occupied him throughout the final decade of his life. At his death in 1969 it remained unfinished, and it was published posthumously in a version edited by Rolf Tiedemann and Gretel Adorno in 1970.[2] It is an important and complex work, and its reception in English-speaking countries was long delayed for lack of a translation.[3] What response there was occurred largely in philosophical journals and monographs, and in historical surveys of the Frankfurt School. Little notice was taken of the book in the field of Anglo-American musicology; this is surprising, given the amount of space Adorno devotes to the discussion of music and music-related problems.

The fragmented and paratactical structure of *Aesthetic Theory* –

---

[1] This essay is based, with modifications, on an article which originally appeared in *Music Analysis* Vol. 6, No. 3 (October 1987), pp.355-77.

[2] Adorno, *Ästhetische Theorie, Gesammelte Schriften* 7 (Frankfurt am Main: Suhrkamp, 1970; 2nd edn, 1972). Page references in this essay are to the Suhrkamp Taschenbuch Wissenschaft edition (1977).

[3] Adorno, *Aesthetic Theory* (1970), trans. by Christian Lenhardt (London: Routledge & Kegan Paul, 1984).

something which is partly intentional but also partly due to the work's incompleteness – renders it remarkably resistant to straightforward summary. The book does not function according to the traditional linear model of initially-stated thesis reasoned through in successive stages. Although this is a characteristic feature of a great deal of Adorno's writing, nowhere within his huge output is it taken to such extremes as in *Aesthetic Theory*.[4] This presents distinct reading difficulties which themselves also need to be understood as an aspect of the book's overall problematic: which is, roughly put, how to write an aesthetics of modernism when the essence of its subject matter, the modernist art work, rejects the kind of systematic, generalized categories and concepts formerly considered indispensable to the discipline of aesthetics and now identified with the *status quo*. While it has been necessary to consider the relationship between the form of *Aesthetic Theory* and its content, and the problems of translation, this essay is mainly devoted to an examination of the approach employed by Adorno in his philosophical interpretation of art and art works, with particular emphasis on music. The intention is to throw into relief the 'method' in Adorno's antisystematic aesthetics by focusing on a limited number of interrelated concepts which may be seen as structural not only to his aesthetics, but also to his sociology of music, and to what he calls his 'immanent analysis' of music. Together this may be seen to constitute Adorno's critical aesthetics of modernism.

This is a risky project, and one likely to attract criticism on the grounds that the style and form of Adorno's writing, its focus on the fragment as critique of totalizing philosophical systems, is actually designed to prevent the kind of approach I am proposing. Although Adorno's dialectical form of argument does not lend

---

[4] In terms of its structure, the book that comes nearest to the form of *Aesthetic Theory* is Adorno's *Minima Moralia* (Frankfurt am Main: Suhrkamp, 1951; English translation by E. F. N. Jephcott, London: NLB, 1974).

itself to reduction, a certain degree of simplification need be no bad thing if it has as its intention the clarification of complex processes in the manner of Max Weber's 'ideal-types'.[5] What is being offered here is a selective and thematic reading of *Aesthetic Theory* in conjunction with other, related texts by Adorno. It could be argued that I am imposing a systematic interpretation which runs counter to the antisystematic style of the texts themselves (where each concept is presented as part of a constellation of ideas, each of which is equidistant from an unstated centre). I would respond that, as a thematic reading, my approach attempts to trace the dynamic shape of only one of these constellations' – that circling around the concept of 'truth content'.[6] At the same time, this approach also brings into focus the methodology underlying Adorno's elliptical manner of presenting his ideas. The contradiction between the antisystematic form of the text and the dialectical method that has shaped it is only apparent. The true contradiction exists in the gap between concepts and their referents, and between totalizing systems and that which they exclude.[7] It is this contradiction that Adorno seeks to reveal in relation to art and

[5] In *Economy and Society* Max Weber writes: 'When we adopt the kind of scientific procedure which involves the construction of types, we can investigate and make fully comprehensible all those irrational, affectively determined, patterns of meaning which influence action, by representing them as "deviations" from a pure type of the action as it would be if it proceeded in a rationally purposive way' (*Weber: Selections in Translation*, ed. W. G. Runciman, trans. Eric Matthews; Cambridge: CUP, 1978, p.9).

[6] Adorno's *Wahrheitsbegriff* is central to his aesthetics. See Friedemann Grenz, 'Zur architektonischen Stellung der Ästhetik in der Philosophie Adornos', in *Theodor W. Adorno: Text + Kritik*, ed. Heinz Ludwig Arnold (Munich: Edition Text + Kritik, 1977), pp.119-29; also, Lambert Zuidervaart, 'Refractions'.

[7] A 'totalizing system' can be understood as any system of thought which claims to represent the whole (for example, the philosophical systems of Kant, Hegel and Marx). Adorno implies that art works and artistic traditions may also be understood as falling under the category of 'totalizing systems – for example, Beethoven and the Austro-German musical tradition, with their emphasis on unity and totality.

aesthetics in his *Aesthetic Theory*, using the dialectical method he had previously developed in relation to philosophy in *Negative Dialectics* (1966),[8] to social theory in *Dialectic of Enlightenment* (with Horkheimer,1944-7)[9] and to immanent musical analysis in *Philosophy of New Music* (1941-9).[10]

1. Modernism, Fragmentation and the Crisis of Meaning

Aesthetic Theory represents the culmination of Adorno's lifelong preoccupation with the philosophical interpretation of works of art and with the critique of traditional formal aesthetic theories. It is an attempt, from what would now be called a 'classical modernist'[11] position, to write an aesthetics of modernism which recognizes at the outset the impossibility of any systematic and unified theory of art today in view of the fragmentation and pluralism which have characterized the art of the twentieth century. At the same time it acknowledges that all thinking about art today still remains inescapably conditioned by (even when operating in opposition to) the harmonistic assumptions handed down from the

[8] Adorno, *Negative Dialectics*, trans. E. B. Ashton (London: Routledge and Kegan Paul, 1973); original German edition, *Negative Dialektik* (Frankfurt am Main: Suhrkamp, 1966).

[9] Adorno, *Dialectic of Enlightenment*, trans. John Cumming (New York: Herder and Herder, 1972; London: NLB, 1979); original German edition, *Dialektik der Aufklärung* (New York, 1947; Frankfurt am Main: Fischer, 1969).

[10] Title translated inaccurately as: Adorno, *Philosophy of Modern Music*, trans. Anne G. Mitchell & Wesley Blomster (New York: Seabury Press, 1973); original German edition, *Philosophie der neuen Musik* (Frankfurt am Main: Europäische Verlagsanstalt, 1949). Referred to throughout this book as *Philosophy of New Music* unless the Mitchell & Blomster translation is being cited directly.

[11] The relevance of Adorno's position to the ongoing debates over postmodernism is nevrtheless clear. See, for example, Habermas, 'Modernity – An Incomplete Project', in *Postmodern Culture*, ed. Hal Foster (London: Pluto, 1985), pp.10-15; and Lyotard, *The Postmodern Condition: A Report on Knowledge*, trans. Geoff Bennington and Brian Massumi, with a Foreword by Fredric Jameson (Manchester: Manchester University, 1984; original French, Editions de Minuit, 1979), pp.72-3. See also pp.40-44 above.

aesthetic traditions of the eighteenth and nineteenth centuries. Adorno's invaluable service has been to reveal the historically and socially mediated nature of all artistic categories, without, however, in the process himself succumbing to some brand of relativism or pluralism. As we have seen, his programme for a Critical Theory, developed with Max Horkheimer and other members of the Frankfurt School in the 1930s, set out to uncover how the relations of power within the capitalist mode of production, and the process of progressive rationalization which has characterized the capitalist period, are reproduced and reflected in apparently autonomous spheres like literature, the visual arts and music. In this, the theory functions as ideology critique. At the same time, however, Critical Theory – and in particular Adorno's own brand of it, 'negative dialectics' – insists that there is something left over in art, a 'surplus' which cannot be reduced to mere ideology. The sphere of art and of aesthetic experience is seen by Adorno as offering a model for emancipation from the dominant mode of instrumental rationality in Western society. The relationship between the social totality and the 'autonomous' realm of art is thus misrepresented if reduced to any crude form of reflectionist theory, or to functionalism. The emphasis is rather on *mediation*; as Adorno puts it: 'Art is mediated by the social totality, more exactly by the dominant structure therein. Its history is not a series of causal relations between two phenomena.[12] The relationship is seen as being infinitely mediated and essentially contradictory, and it is the mapping and deciphering of the traces and gaps left in the apparent unity of autonomous art works and in aesthetic systems by the unreconciled tension between art and social reality that are the locus of Adorno's *Aesthetic Theory* (and indeed of all his writings on aesthetics and the sociology of art).

[12] Adorno, *Aesthetic Theory*, p.300.

The Task of Aesthetics and the Crisis of Meaning

In the opening lines of *Aesthetic Theory* Adorno indicates that it is the loss of certainty and the 'crisis of meaning' in art today that presents contemporary aesthetics with its task: 'What has become self-evident is that nothing concerning art is any longer self-evident – not in terms of itself, not in terms of its relation to the whole, and not even in terms of its very right to exist'.[13] Thus for Adorno the basic task of a theoretical aesthetics of modernism is to explain, clarify and explicate the terms of this dilemma. 'Art is waiting to be explicated', he insists;[14] indeed, he considers that art works demand explication in order to be understood at all. In a series of lectures on aesthetics he gave at Frankfurt University during 1967-8, while engaged in the writing of *Aesthetic Theory*, Adorno further expanded on the nature of such explication. He saw its purpose as twofold: 1) to interpret the art work (both in terms of 'immanent analysis' and in terms of the relation to society); and 2) to develop the concept of understanding itself in relation to art works.[15] In other words, aesthetics had to become a self-reflective – and thus critical – theoretical activity; a dialectical aesthetics aiming to interpret on the one hand the art work (both as 'autonomous monad' and as socially mediated fact) and on the other hand the theoretical method of approach itself and its underlying assumptions. Philosophizing about art and the nature of the aesthetic experience therefore becomes itself the object of critical enquiry; it becomes historically situated, and the relationship to dominant ideologies also comes under focus.

According to Adorno, the historical reason for this dual emphasis, dating from the kind of self-questioning characteristic

[13] Adorno, *Ästhetische Theorie*, p.9 (my translation); cf. *Aesthetic Theory*, p.1.
[14] Adorno, *Aesthetic Theory*, p. 484.
[15] See Adorno, *Vorlesungen zur Ästhetik* (1967-68) (Zurich: Mayer, 1973), pp.1-6. This is a pirated edition of Adorno's 1967-8 lecture series on aesthetics, published in typescript with many of the lectures incomplete.

of the avant-garde art work since Baudelaire,[16] is that one of the most fundamental assumptions of traditional aesthetics has been thrown into doubt: the assumption that it is possible to understand art works at all, at least in the limited sense of closed meanings. For, he maintains, it is precisely understanding (*Verstehen*) and intelligibility (*Verständlichkeit*) which have become radically problematic in modern art and which are now, as a 'complex of problems', thematic to it. In other words, 'unintelligibility' becomes itself a structuring principle of the avant-garde art work of the 'classical modernist' period, presenting itself as a formal problem which demands interpretation and understanding, but which at the same time refuses to allow the contradictions presented by its form to be reconciled. Thus, although the modernist art work, like the art of the past, is in need of an appropriate aesthetics to complement it, it is not the task of aesthetics to explain away this 'moment of unintelligibility' so intrinsic to what Adorno regards as authentic modern art, and to excise its element of strangeness, as these moments constitute in themselves a considerable part of the content of modernist art works. The task of a philosophical aesthetics is rather, as Adorno put it in his 1967-8 lecture series on aesthetics, 'to understand this unintelligibility: why these art works deny themselves intelligibility in the sense of a discursive surface context of meaning'.[17]

Form and the Modernist Dilemma

This brings us to the central stylistic and formal problematic of *Aesthetic Theory* itself. Although the book is not exclusively

---

[16] Like Walter Benjamin, Adorno dates the emergence of aesthetic modernism and the avant garde from Baudelaire. In *Aesthetic Theory* Adorno writes: 'Baudelaire's poetry was the first to express the fact that art in a fully developed commodity society can do nothing except look on powerlessly as that society drifts along. The only way in which art can henceforth transcend the heteronomy of capitalist society is by suffusing its own autonomy with the imagery of that society' (p.31).

[17] Adorno, *Vorlesungen*, p.1.

occupied with modern art, it is nevertheless clear that the underlying theme is the dilemma of modernism, and that the extensive
discussion of earlier art and aesthetic theories is conducted
always in terms of the relationship to the position of the avant
garde. The dilemma of modernism as Adorno understands it
may be defined briefly as the predicament faced by the artist
caught between, on the one hand, the traditional demands of the
art work for unity and integration (the harmonious relationship
between part and whole) and, on the other hand, the loss of faith
in any overarching unity on both individual and social levels in
the face of the evident fragmentation of modern existence
(manifesting as critical opposition to the 'false totality' of the
status quo, represented by the culture industry). Aesthetics today,
according to Adorno, has the problem of understanding 'a
situation where art revolts against its essential concepts while at
the same time being inconceivable without them'.[18] This
problem – how to evolve structures which can admit chaos,
fragmentation and meaninglessness and which at the same time,
through 'critical consciousness', can transcend such content – is
central to both content and form of *Aesthetic Theory*.

The Open Structure of Aesthetic Theory
One immediate result of this is a book of enormous complexity,
a complexity which Adorno clearly saw as an inescapable aspect
of his subject matter, the modernist art work. Adorno is quoted
by his editors as writing:

> Interestingly the content of thoughts has, for me, a bearing on their
> form. I knew and expected this all along. But now that it has hap-
> pened I am dumbfounded all the same. My theorem that there is no
> philosophical 'first thing' is coming back to haunt me. Much as I
> might be tempted, I cannot now proceed to construct a universe of
> reasoning in the usual orderly fashion. Instead I have to put together

[18] Adorno, *Aesthetic Theory*, p. 465.

a whole from a series of partial complexes which are concentrically complexes which are concentrically arranged and have the same weight and relevance. It is the constellation, not the succession one by one of these partial complexes which has to make sense.[19]

Nevertheless, the book is also fragmentary because Adorno died before he could finish it. The editors are firm on this point:

> As it is, the book remains a torso. . . . Adorno's argument that 'the fragmentary quality of a work becomes part of its expression' (because it expresses the criticism of totality and systematicity which is so much a part of his philosophy) obviating the illusion necessarily perpetuated by spirit – this argument is unconvincing in view of the destruction to which the text of *Aesthetic Theory* attests. The concept of fragment has a double meaning for Adorno. It can refer to something productive: for systematic theories to disclose their truth content they must disintegrate into fragments. This is not true of *Aesthetic Theory*. It is fragmentary in another sense; we are dealing here with death's tampering with a work before it had realised its inherent law of form.[20]

The editors have therefore presented the drafts left by Adorno in a form which does not try to hide the work's incompleteness, but which at the same time attempts to group the material according to some coherent plan. In the form in which he left the work Adorno had dispensed with all chapter divisions and section headings (something which the editors have respected in the German edition, but which the translator into English has not). The editors have organized the material into twelve large sections, and at the end have added, as 'Paralipomena', 154 shorter fragments which it was difficult to place with any certainty within the main body of the text, but which Adorno had intended to incorporate. Also included is a longer section

[19] Adorno, *Aesthetic Theory*, Editors' Epilogue, p.496.
[20] Ibid., pp.493–4.

entitled 'Theories on the Origin of Art'; and finally there is a draft of an introduction to the whole work.

The editors' decision not to attempt to 'complete' the book was undoubtedly the correct one, and their warning against 'any attempt at squeezing some metaphysical meaning out of the fact of death'[21] in view of the work's open structure needs to be borne in mind. Nevertheless, between the evidence of Adorno's intentions concerning the final form of the book, and the incompleteness of the realization of those intentions, the reader is faced with even greater difficulties than the usual ones associated with Frankfurt School texts. And if this were not enough, these difficulties are compounded in translation.

Translation Problems

Strangely in line with Adorno's own metaphor of avant-garde art works as messages in bottles thrown into the sea,[22] the publication of the translation of *Aesthetic Theory* seemed to pass relatively unnoticed in the field of music theory when the book was washed up on Anglo-American shores.[23] It is tempting to ascribe this lack of impact, at least in part, to the general untranslatability of Adorno's prose. On one level one is full of admiration for a translator prepared to take on such a difficult and lengthy text, and who manages to come up with something which is at least readable. However, a closer reading in conjunction with the original often reveals disturbing tendencies to go in for paraphrase and approximation. I have discussed particular translation issues in some detail elsewhere.[24] What is relevant here, however, is the question

[21] Ibid., pp.494.

[22] '[New music] is truly the message in a bottle thrown into the sea by the shipwrecked' [*Sie ist die wahre Flaschenpost.*] (*Philosophie der neuen Musik, Gesammelte Schriften* 12, ed. Rolf Tiedemann (Frankfurt: Suhrkamp Verlag, 1975) p.126).

[23] The most thorough review of *Aesthetic Theory* is Bob Hullot-Kentor, 'Adorno's *Aesthetic Theory*: The Translation', *Telos*, No. 65 (Fall 1985).

[24] See original version of this essay, Max Paddison, 'Adorno's *Aesthetic Theory*'.

of the precise translation of central and recurring concepts. The thorniest of these are the familiar ones like *Geist*[25] and *Aufhebung*,[26] for which there are no adequate or unambiguous English equivalents. Here the translation fares no better and no worse than other attempts to deal with Hegelian-type texts, and the usual confusion follows. Others for which more adequate solutions could have been found are important concepts like *Entkunstung*, translated as 'desubstantialization' but which could be more adequately rendered as 'de-aestheticization',[27] and the difficult distinction between *Inhalt* and *Gehalt*, both of which can be translated as 'content', depending on the context. Very often, however, the same concept is translated by two or more different terms in different contexts in the English version, without any acknowledgment of this (that is, with the German term included immediately afterwards in brackets). This creates unnecessary confusion, for it is precisely the concepts in Adorno's writing (as in any philosophical and sociological texts) that provide the essential reference points by which one is able to orientate oneself within otherwise perpetually shifting theoretical contexts.

Sympathy is due to any translator faced with Adorno's prose. However, in the interests of accessibility the translation of *Aesthetic Theory* tends to conceal the essential complexity of the original, and with it at times the implicit dialectical method which

[25] That *Geist* has to be translated as 'spirit', 'mind' or 'intellect', none of which really captures the sense of the German concept, is a problem. In the context of Adorno's *Aesthetic Theory* it should, as a general rule, be translated as 'spirit'.

[26] *Aufhebung* is perhaps one of the most difficult of all dialectical concepts to translate. If translated as 'negation', it becomes confused with Adorno's concept of *Negation* (as in *bestimmte Negation*); if translated as 'cancelling', the sense of opposites being synthesized' at a new qualitative level and becoming the thesis of a new dialectical interaction is lost. 'Sublation' is better, but there is no real solution to the problem: the concept needs a lengthy footnote to itself in the context of philosophical prose.

[27] See the extended discussion of the concept of *Entkunstung* in Wolin, 'The De-aestheticization of Art'.

is inscribed in the text.[28] While it is undesirable to make a fetish out of complexity for its own sake, it is necessary in Adorno's case to recognize that the complexity of his style is in part derived from a very calculated use of contradiction. This, in turn, is made possible by the peculiar potential retained by the German language for formulating dialectical thought.[29] This potential lies both in the syntax of the language and in the way in which philosophical concepts are so easily formed out of everyday words.[30] Although Adorno exploits this tendency to an extreme not reached even by Hegel, this is nevertheless done against the background of a philosophical and poetic tradition which has long made play with the ambiguities and contradictions inherent in the German language and which are seen as a reflection of the ambiguity and ultimate inaccessibility of the object 'in itself'. A concrete vocabulary is combined with a rational grammatical structure to build abstract and totalizing systems of thought dedicated to the grasping of elusive metaphysical truths. The essence of the Idealist tradition could be summarized as the attempt to grasp the non-conceptual by means of the concept, a position further extended – and criticized – by Adorno through his negative dialectics. However, the very attempt to formulate in English such a rationale for Adorno's idiosyncratic use of the German language – emphasizing as it does an element of the Absurd of which Adorno was certainly aware[31]

---

[28] For the translator's response to criticisms, see Christian Lenhardt, 'Reply to Hullot-Kentor', *Telos*, No. 65 (Fall 1985).

[29] Samuel Weber, 'Translating the Untranslatable', in Adorno, *Prisms: Cultural Criticism and Society*, trans. Samuel and Shierry Weber (London: Neville Spearman, 1967).

[30] The tendency of English to translate German philosophical concepts (which frequently have their roots in everyday 'concrete' vocabulary) by resorting to words that derive from Latin or Greek roots is epitomized by the standard translation of *Verdinglichung* as 'reification'.

[31] 'The literature of the absurd shares in the following dialectic, at least as far as its greatest exponents are concerned: in order to express the fact that there is no meaning it makes use of teleological organization and a complex of meaning. In so doing the literature of the absurd keeps alive the category of meaning in

– serves to highlight the deeply-rooted differences between the two languages, and further emphasizes the problem of translation itself. In reflecting upon and attempting to explicate the 'crisis of meaning' in art today, Adorno is simultaneously using language, the written word, against itself (in a manner not unlike that of Samuel Beckett, to whom *Aesthetic Theory* was to have been dedicated), in order to reveal the gap between the word and that to which it refers. Samuel Weber writes:

> The unresolved tension which shapes an Adorno sentence, aphorism, essay, book, from beginning to end, lives from and bears witness to the impossibility of a harmonious union of form and content, language and meaning, an idea which survives in his work precisely in and through its determinate negation... The untranslatability of Adorno is his most profound and cruel truth. What remains is not the saturated unity of language and meaning but their disjunction, 'allegorical' in the sense given to the word by Walter Benjamin.[32]

2. Truth-Content, Authenticity and Musical Self-Reflection

Adorno's use of the concepts 'truth' and 'truth content' in relation to art, and in particular in relation to music as essentially the most non-conceptual of all modes of art, appears, on the surface at least, decidedly obscure. This is due in part to the deliberately fragmented way in which he presents his ideas, as discussed above. However, without a more precise understanding of these concepts the motive force behind his notion of the 'dialectic of musical

[31] *(cont.)*
determinate negation. That is what makes its interpretation possible, indeed worthwhile' (*Aesthetic Theory*, p.225).

[32] Samuel M. Weber, 'Translating the Untranslatable', in T.W. Adorno, *Prisms*, trans. Samuel and Shierry Weber (London: Neville Spearman, 1967), pp.14–15.

material' will also remain mysterious and the criteria underlying his value judgments will appear arbitrary – if not at times dogmatic and prejudiced. That Adorno's dialectical approach to aesthetics is value-laden is not in dispute; he himself is quite clear on this point when he writes in *Aesthetic Theory*: 'The idea of a value-neutral aesthetics is nonsense'.[33] Furthermore, that his notions of value, quality and authenticity are directly related to the 'truth content' of the work of art is revealed when in *Philosophy of New Music* he cites Hegel: 'For in human art we are not merely dealing with playthings, however pleasant or useful they may be, but . . . with a revelation of truth'.[34] An examination of key moments which constitute for Adorno the concept of 'truth content', to be found scattered throughout his writings, may therefore contribute to an understanding of this problematical notion.

Adorno's Concept of Art

Adorno's concept of art, as part of his larger social and philosophical theory, is culturally specific, in that it refers to high art in Western industrialized society. It also needs to be understood in relation to his notion of the avant garde, and is defined negatively through its dynamic relation to what lies outside its concept – for instance, society, nature:

> Art . . . is different from empirical reality. Now this difference itself does not stay the same; it changes because art changes. History, for example, has transformed certain cult objects into art long after they were first produced. Or, to give another example, at a certain moment in time particular art objects have ceased to be viewed as art. In this connection the abstractly posed question of whether a phenomenon like film is art or something else is instructive, although it leads nowhere. . . . Art has a changing scope, and it

[33] Adorno. *Aesthetic Theory*, p.371.
[34] Adorno, *Philosophy of Modern Music*, p.3.
[35] Adorno, *Aesthetic Theory*, p.3.

may be just as well not to try to define sharply what's inside and what's outside of it.[35]

For Adorno the concept of art 'balks at being defined, for it is a historically changing constellation of moments. Nor can the nature of art be ascertained by going back to the origin of art in order to find some fundamental and primary layer that supports everything else'.[36] Art cannot be defined in terms of what it once was, as it is also a process of *becoming*, proceeding by way of *negation* of its own previously-existing concept. Although it is dependent upon tradition and derived from it, it proceeds through critique and negation of prevailing historical and social norms within its own material. In this, it is involved in a process of constant redefinition and expansion of its own reified concept at any particular historical period. As a mode of 'non-conceptual cognition' art employs extreme rationality, in terms of the logicality of its form and in terms of its relation to technique and technology, as critique of the means-ends rationality of society. Since its emancipation from direct social function, and in particular from its association with cult and magic, art has itself become part of the 'dialectic of Enlightenment'. As Adorno puts it, 'art is part and parcel of the disenchantment of the world, to use Max Weber's term. It is inextricably entwined with rationalization'.[37] At the same time, Adorno considers, the rationality of art is inseparable from its mimetic aspect – *mimesis* here to be understood not as direct imitation or representation of the outside world, but rather as a non-conceptual, possibly gestural 'identifying with' on the part of the subject which traces the dynamic laws of the object.[38] Mimesis and rationality are seen by Adorno as irreconcilable and

[35] Adorno, *Aesthetic Theory*, p.3.
[36] Ibid.
[37] Ibid., p.80.
[38] See Michael Cahn, 'Subversive Mimesis: Theodor W. Adorno and the Modern Impasse of Critique', in *Mimesis in Contemporary Theory*, Vol. 1, ed. Mihai Spariosu (Philadelphia: Benjamin, 1984), p.34.

yet dependent upon each other, constituting the inner dialectic of the art work as, for example, the dialectic of expression and construction. The tension generated by the art work, as a force-field, is the result of a conflict between the mimetic impulse, 'blind expression', which threatens to fall back into magic, and rationality as construction, the logic of form, which is the self-reflective aspect of the work and which threatens the blind quality of the work with disenchantment and enlightenment. It is the tension between these two moments (which Adorno sees as an essential aspect of autonomous art works) which gives to art both its language-character (*Sprachcharakter*)[39] and its riddle-character (*Rätselcharakter*): 'that art works say something and in the same breath hide it puts their riddle-character under the aspect of language. There is something clown-like about it...'.[40] This paradoxical quality of art works – their enigma, which has charac-teristics of the *Vexierbild*, a puzzle which has a potential but not a final solution – is that in them which demands philosophical interpretation: that is to say, 'interpretative understanding' in the sense of Max Weber's use of the term *Verstehen*.[41]

Adorno maintains that it is via the dialectic of mimesis and

[39] See Max Paddison, 'The Language-Character of Music: Some Motifs in Adorno', Journal of the Royal Musical Association 116/2 (1991), pp.267-79.

[40] Adorno, *Ästhetische Theorie*, p.182 (my translation); cf. Aesthetic Theory, p. 176.

[41] Gillian Rose writes that Adorno 'takes Weber's definition of sociological inquiry at the beginning of *Economy and Society*, as the interpretation of subject-ively meaningful social action (*Verstehen*) to be a Substantive and prescriptive thesis that social action should be intelligible as the realisation of men's will, as rational. Weber's instruction to unpack social institutions so as to reveal the individual's orientation to them is not merely a methodological device but a theory of what constitutes autonomy. Men are free and social institutions are rational to the extent that they express men's will and are understood to do so, to the extent that they are transparent. In a society in which social relations between men are determined by the production of value in exchange, the social institu-tions which arise cannot be intelligible in the sense specified because of commod-ity fetishism' (*The Melancholy Science: An Introduction to the Thought of Theodor W. Adorno*, London: Macmillan, 1978, p.82).

rationality that the outside world enters the hermetic world of the art work – not directly, but in mediated form. Society, as collectivity, penetrates the work through, for example, historically and socially mediated musical material, through the process of rationalization which it both takes from the instrumental rationality of society and at the same time opposes, and through the mimetic impulse which imitates the dynamic movement of the outside world but which also expresses resistance to it. It is therefore possible, in summary, to identify three different aspects which constitute Adorno's concept of art: (1) art is different from and opposes society; (2) art is derived from and part of society; (3) art points beyond society.[42] These three aspects of art are complemented by the three levels of analysis, critique and interpretation presented at the end of this chapter. Thus it is apparent that for Adorno the 'truth content' of the art work – the correspondence of the work to that which lies outside its 'monad-like' existence as individual object – possesses both subjective and objective moments, as does the work itself.

Truth Content and the Priority of the Object

For Adorno, truth lies in the Object; it is not merely a projection of the thinking Subject. Nevertheless, the truth content of the work of art as object can only be revealed through philosophical interpretation: that is, via the pre-existent knowledge and experience that the Subject brings to bear upon it.[43] Philosophical

---

[42] See Lambert Zuidervaart, 'Adorno, Aesthetic Theory' [review], *The Journal of Aesthetics and Art Theory*, Vol. 44, No. 2 (Winter 1985). Zuidervaart writes: 'According to Adorno's methodological principle, the development of modern art suggests the following general thesis: art derives from a larger social process, opposes and points beyond it, but remains part of that process' (p.195). This general thesis is applied by Adorno not only to 'modern art' but to the whole development of autonomous art in the 'bourgeois period'.

[43] See Adorno, 'Types of Musical Conduct', in *Introduction to the Sociology of Music*, trans. E. B. Ashton (New York: Seabury, 1976), concerning 'structural listening' and the 'expert listener' (pp.4-5).

interpretation seeks first, via immanent analysis, to describe as closely as possible the inner dialectic of the work itself (its structure, the relation of parts to whole, the development of its material), and then to interpret the dialectic of subjective expression and objective technique which constitutes the work, via 'sociological analysis', in terms of the social content of the work and how this reflects the dialectic of society. In this sense, Adorno maintains, art may itself be understood as a form of social theory – mute, however, until brought to speech via philosophical interpretation and aesthetic evaluation. The prioritizing of the Object in philosophical terms has its parallel in Adorno's sociology of music. Here the emphasis is on the sphere of production (and furthermore on the forces of production rather than on the relations of production). The spheres of distribution and reception/ consumption are regarded as contingent because, Adorno maintains, restriction to the sphere of reception/ consumption 'would endanger objective cognition . . . because the effects of works of art and of intellectual creations in general are not absolute and final, and cannot be satisfactorily determined by recourse to the recipients. Rather, the effects depend on innumerable mechanisms of distribution, of social control and authority, and finally on the social structure, within which the determining relations can be ascertained'.[44] The social function of the musical work, and the context of effects in which it finds itself, are important for Adorno only insofar as they affect musical content. 'Art and society converge in content (*Gehalt*)', he insists, 'not in something external to the work of art'.[45]

[44] Adorno, 'Theses on the Sociology of Art' (1967), trans. Brian Trench, *Birmingham Working Papers in Cultural Studies 2* (1972), p.121.

[45] Adorno, *Ästhetische Theorie*, p.339 (my translation); cf. *Aesthetic Theory*, p.324. Lenhardt is correct in translating *Gehalt* as 'substance'; however, the sense of 'content' also needs to be conveyed.

Truth Content and the Emancipation of the Subject

That the truth content of the musical work and the emancipation of the Subject are closely linked for Adorno is made clear when, in passing, he defines truth content in *Aesthetic Theory* as 'the voice of the Subject's coming of age, emancipation from myth and reconcilement with it'.[46] Examination of works of the 'bourgeois period' (the period roughly from the early eighteenth century to the twentieth century) reveals an undeniable progress in terms of technique, Adorno maintains. The 'dialectic of musical material' – essentially the dialectic of expressive needs and technical means – is on one level an account of this technical progress. He writes: 'There is no question that materials and the mastery over them – technique in the narrow sense – advances historically'.[47] As examples of this across the arts he gives 'the invention of perspective in painting and that of polyphony in music'.[48] He also goes on to say that this progress is characterized by increasing rationalization of artistic procedures: 'There is no denying either that progress also occurs within already established procedures, such progress being a movement towards increasing logical elaboration'.[49] As examples of this he gives 'the growing differentiation of harmonic perception between the thorough-bass period and the beginnings of modern music, or the passage from impressionism to pointillism in painting'.[50] But, Adorno insists, progress in technique and in rationalization of artistic procedures 'does not necessarily entail progress in artistic quality'.[51] Progress in quality and authenticity – finally in terms of truth content – 'is also the progress of spirit (*Geist*) in the Hegelian

---

[46] Adorno, *Ästhetische Theorie*, p.316 (my translation); cf. *Aesthetic Theory*, p.303.

[47] Adorno, *Aesthetic Theory*, p.300.

[48] Ibid.

[49] Ibid.

[50] Ibid.

[51] Ibid., p.301.

sense of the term, i.e., an increasing awareness by spirit of its freedom'.[52]

The Dialectic of Musical Material

The goal of the dialectic of musical material, or its driving force, is seen by Adorno to be the articulation of the expressive Subject, of *Geist*, as objectified in musical structures. The 'plot' is the historically increasing awareness by the expressive Subject of the nature of the demands upon it coming from the musical material – and, as the material is regarded by Adorno not as being of purely 'natural' origin but as a 'sedimentation' of historical and social tendencies, these musical/compositional demands are also social demands.[53] Hence Adorno's insistence on the priority of the Object – the musical work analysed immanently, in its own terms. As he said in a talk given in 1969, 'On the Problem of Musical Analysis', 'the work of art insists that we put this question of truth or untruth immanently and not arbitrarily bring some yardstick or other of the cultural-philosophical or cultural-critical varieties to the work from outside'.[54] However, this assertion of Adorno's does need qualifying here, as the objection could well be raised that he himself has brought an external yardstick in the form of Frankfurt-style Critical Theory to bear on autonomous music, in order to decipher its truth content. Indeed, it is quite clear that the entire value system embodied in his music theory, including his concept of musical material, is but a special application of the broader social theory of the Frankfurt School, especially as formulated in *Dialectic of Enlightenment*. What it is important to recognize here is that the larger theoretical framework employed by Adorno is consistently present in his work, is not 'hidden' and is

[52] Ibid., p.303.

[53] For Adorno' s account of his concept of 'musical material' [*Materialbegriff*], see *Philosophy of Modern Music*, pp. 32-7.

[54] Adorno, 'On the Problem of Musical Analysis', trans. and introduced by Max Paddison, *Music Analysis*, Vol. 1, No.2 (July 1982), p.177.

acknowledged by him at every turn. In fact, without some familiarity with the terms of reference of Critical Theory and its background it is doubtful whether Adorno can be understood at all.[55] The general point made by Horkheimer in his essay 'On the Problem of Truth' is relevant here: 'Separated from a particular theory of society as a whole, every theory of cognition remains formalistic and abstract.'[56]

Self-Reflection of the Musical Work

Adorno maintains that the musical work of the bourgeois period, regarded as a 'context of meaning', a mode of non–conceptual cognition, becomes, paralleling social and philosophical theory, increasingly self-reflective. The form this self-reflection takes in the technical structure of works of art consists in their turning against the previously accepted canon of meanings encapsulated within their material, in terms of musical conventions as handed down historically. Adorno sees it as a process of increasing critique and rejection of the positive, affirmative meanings traditionally associated with art, to the point of the negation of meaning itself. The reasons for this negation of meaning are not to be discovered merely in the conscious intentions of the artist. The causes are historical and social in origin, and their effects constitute the social content of such art (Adorno is again referring to the avant garde – that art at the most advanced stage of the dialectic of expressive needs and technical means). One of the effects of this historical process has been, according to Adorno, the retreat of art into its own formal problems, into apparent meaninglessness (in the sense of a rejection of conventions, of consensus) and into a

[55] The most useful historical introduction to the Critical Theory of the Frankfurt School is Jay, *The Dialectical Imagination*.

[56] Max Horkheimer, 'On the Problem of Truth', in *The Essential Frankfurt School Reader*, ed. Andrew Arato and Eike Gebhardt (Oxford: Blackwell, 1978), pp.426-7. This essay originally appeared in German in *Zeitschrift für Sozialforschung*, Vol. 4 (1935).

purposelessness which has been an aspect of its 'autonomy character'[57] since the beginning of the bourgeois period. Adorno explains this in *Aesthetic Theory* as follows:

> Works of art are purposeless in the sense of being removed from reality and from useful personal strategies of survival. It is precisely for this reason that we speak of 'meaning' rather than 'purpose' [*Zweck*] in art, despite the patent affinities that exist between meaning and the immanent teleology of purpose. Historically, the difficulties that art has had in projecting a complex of meaning have been growing worse. The ultimate response to this situation is to deny the very idea of meaning, a response we see today in various forms. As the emancipation of the subject demolished an ever greater number of constructs of a pre-established, meaningful order, the concept of meaning began to lose its plausibility in theology as well. Theology had been meaning's last refuge. But it was an affirmative lie to try and ascribe positive meaning to life. A lie it was already, long before Auschwitz: earlier historical developments already pointed in this direction.[58]

The negation of meaning in such works does not signify that they are therefore irrelevant and without meaning. Their 'nothingness' is to be understood positively, *ein positives Negativum*, as Adorno calls it, which serves to raise the whole issue of meaning once more to the status of a problem in the age of modernity – without, however, putting any positive meaning in its place.

Authenticity and Quality
Adorno distinguishes between two different responses to the crisis of meaning: (1) *authentic art*, 'which engages the crisis of meaning ...in which the negation of meaning takes shape as a negative

---

[57] See Chapter 1.
[58] Adorno, *Aesthetic Theory*, p.219.

quality' and is meaningful;[59] and (2) *resigned art*, 'which consists literally and figuratively, of positivistic protocol sentences', where meaninglessness is simply mirrored without self-reflection, and where 'the negation of meaning . . . represents an adaptation to the *status quo*', is 'immediate, and bypasses the subject'.[60] This categorization corresponds to the distinction Adorno makes in *Negative Dialectics* between, on the one hand, non–identity thinking, the negation of the concept by the concept (in art, the negation of traditional meaning and rationality by means of rationally organized 'emptiness' or obscurity), and, on the other hand, identity thinking, the positive affirmation of the total identity of concept and reality (in art, the simple and uncritical reflection of the status quo). Nevertheless, in spite of its negation of meaning in terms of traditional categories and artistic procedures, 'authentic' art in this sense cannot help but, at the same time, posit meaning – if only because art cannot escape, of its very nature, being loaded with significance. However fragmented it may be, a work of art is still perceived as a unity – or at least as a fragment of an implied whole. What constitutes the truth and quality of 'authentic' art for Adorno is the extent to which it retains this contradiction unreconciled within its structure and confronts it. Adorno described this in a discussion with the Marxist culture critic Lucien Goldmann:

> I would say that the rank or the quality of works of art is measured – if one can employ this flat term – according to the degree in which antagonisms are formed within the work of art, and in which their unity is attained through antagonisms rather than remaining external to them.[61]

[59] Ibid., p.221.
[60] Ibid.
[61] Adorno and Goldmann, 'To Describe, Understand and Explain', in Lucien Goldmann, *Cultural Creation in Modern Society*, trans. Bart Grahl (St Louis: Telos, 1976), Appendix 3, p. 145.

From this it becomes clear that Adorno is quite specific in his use of concepts like authenticity and quality in art works, and that, seen within the framework of his broader aesthetic (and social) theory, these value-laden and rather perilous terms do take on a more precise meaning. In this context, therefore, he is using the concept authenticity (*Authentizität*) in a very different sense from its current use in connection with (a) the performance of early music (a critique of which he offered in his essay 'Bach Defended against His Devotees' in *Prisms*);[62] and (b) German existential philosophy (his book *The Jargon of Authenticity*[63] is a critique of the notion of *Eigentlichkeit* – also translated into English as 'authenticity' – in the work of existentialists like Buber, Jaspers and, in particular, Heidegger). Adorno's notion of authenticity is founded on the idea of appropriate responses to the changing historically and socially mediated demands of the material of art. It thus at the same time operates as a critique of those ahistorical notions of authenticity which are based on ideas of unmediated 'pure being' (*Sein*) or ultimate origins.

3. Analysis, Critique and Interpretation

Although Adorno was critical of any rigid division of intellectual labour into strictly separated disciplines, and tended to move, for example, between technical analysis, sociology and philosophy of music as seemed appropriate, he was at the same time quite clear as to the individual contribution of each discipline. It was, however, because of his awareness of the limitations of each of these approaches in isolation, and his insistence that concepts are never totally adequate to the object of thought, that he felt the

[62] Adorno, 'Bach Defended against His Devotees', Prisms, pp. 133–46.

[63] Adorno, *The Jargon of Authenticity*, trans. Knut Tarnowski and Frederick Will (London: Routledge and Kegan Paul, 1973); original German edition, *Jargon der Eigentlichkeit: Zur deutschen Ideologie* (Frankfurt am Main: Suhrkamp, 1964).

need to develop an interdisciplinary theory which, as he put it, 'must strive, by way of the concept, to transcend the concept',[64] in order to arrive back at an understanding of the object (in this case the work of art) in all its unfamiliarity and contradictoriness. Adorno considered the intellectual division of labour to be both artificial and distorting, particularly in relation to sociology:

> The division of labour between disciplines such as philosophy, sociology, psychology and history is not contained in their material, but has been forced upon them from outside. The call for interdisciplinary methods is especially valid in sociology, which in a certain sense extends over all possible subjects. As social consciousness it should aim to put right something of the social wrong which has inflicted this division of labour on consciousness.[65]

There is a sense in which all the disciplines on which Adorno draws can be subsumed under the umbrella of his 'aesthetics, in that they all terminate for him in questions of value and aesthetic judgment, and ultimately in the question of truth content. This has inevitably led to complaints that his sociology of music is not really sociology at all, but rather an extension of his value-laden aesthetics into the social domain. K.P. Etzkorn has suggested that 'Adorno approaches the sociology of music with an implicit program in mind . . . it is not to study music and its relation to man in an objective manner, but to pronounce a system of values; and to find substantiation for these values is the aim of his sociology'.[66] It also has to be conceded that his so-called 'immanent analyses' of musical works are disappointingly traditional on a technical level, and do not convincingly bridge the gap between technical analysis and philosophical interpretation. Diether de la Motte, for

[64] Adorno, *Negative Dialectics*, p.15.
[65] Adorno, 'Theses on the Sociology of Art', p. 127.
[66] K.P. Etzkorn, 'Sociologists and Music', in *Music and Society: The Later Writings of Paul Honigsheim*, ed. K. P. Etzkorn (New York: Wiley, 1973), p.23.

example, has argued that Adorno's music analyses are rather limited and schematic.[67] And finally, Adorno's philosophy of music, in striving to transcend the concept and dissolve itself in the art object, becomes dangerously akin to art itself – no longer philosophy, but rather a form of poetic speculation on the nature of art, trapped within a circle of endless negations. These are valid criticisms, whether they stem from a tradition of Anglo–Saxon empiricism or from more orthodox varieties of Marxist theory than Adorno's own idiosyncratic brand of Hegelian-Marxism; they will be returned to at the end of this essay and also in Chapter 4. On another level, however, such criticisms need not be taken as the damning indictments they may at first appear. Providing it is possible to concede that Adorno's hermeneutic approach to the aesthetics, sociology and analysis of music does lead to valid insights – however fragmented – into the nature and problems of the art object and of aesthetic experience in Western industrialized society, then the lacunae and blind spots which any thorough-going critique of his work reveals can also be taken as areas calling for further critical development. In this Adorno's *Aesthetic Theory* can be understood as an incomplete project in more senses than the merely literal.[68]

The following model is a drawing together of two apparently contradictory processes: (i) fragmented references to 'truth content' scattered throughout Adorno's writings are synthesized; and (ii) different levels of analysis, critique and interpretation which are fused – and consciously so – in Adorno's work are separated and highlighted for heuristic purposes. By separating out these levels I hope to demonstrate the dialectical relationship between them and indicate the method underlying them. This acts as one attempt to make explicit what is implicit in Adorno's work. While my emphasis is on its particular application to music, the

---

[67] For a critique of Adorno's technical analyses see Diether de la Motte, 'Adornos musikalische Analysen', in *Adorno und die Musik*, ed. Otto Kolleritsch (Graz: Universal, 1979). Also Max Paddison, *Adorno's Aesthetics of Music*.

[68] See also Max Paddison, *Adorno's Aesthetics of Music*, pp.276–8.

broader application of the model to art in general is clear enough from the generality of the concepts used.

A Dialectical Model

We are concerned here with the three levels of analysis outlined above:

1. immanent (including technical) analysis
2. sociological critique
3. philosophical-historical interpretation

Each of these levels can be understood in relation to a focal concept in Adorno's aesthetics which points to a particular notion of the 'truth' or 'untruth' of musical works. That is to say, crudely put: (1) technical analysis seeks to reveal the structural *consistency* of the musical work in relation to its dominating musical 'idea'; (2) sociological critique seeks to uncover the *ideology* of the musical work in relation to its social context; and (3) philosophical-historical interpretation seeks to identify the *authenticity* of the musical work in terms of the solution of particular formal problems in relation to the demands of the socially and historically determined musical material.

The dialectical relationship between these three interacting levels can be represented diagrammatically as follows:

(1) *consistency* ⟶ o ⟵ (2) *ideology*

(the musical work understood as autonomous, self-consistent, self-contained text)

(the 'autonomy' of the musical work seen as ideological through situating it in its social context as a commodity)

(3) *authenticity*

(the degree to which the musical work's unity of form is attained through antagonisms, through the conflict between its 'autonomy character' and its 'commodity character')

(o = oppositional relationship)

Adorno tends to work on these three levels simultaneously, although the emphasis certainly varies considerably depending on the particular focus of any individual piece of work. This multiple emphasis, or rapid oscillation between levels, is responsible for much misunderstanding of Adorno's writings on aesthetics and on music in particular. It is important, therefore, that the levels be clearly distinguished theoretically in order to grasp their constant interaction within Adorno's critical aesthetics.

(1)The version of truth content which focuses on *consistency* implies a form of nominalism, each work uniquely itself and functioning as a hermetically-sealed system of relationships. The work is more or less logically consistent with its own definition of itself, in terms of intention, 'idea', rational structure, etc. Adorno, however, works with a dialectical notion of truth, derived from Hegelian logic, which argues that truth lies not only in the identity of concept and object but also in their *non–identity*. That is to say, objects are defined not only in terms of what they *are*, but also in terms of what they *are not* – by what is excluded by the concept, by what is 'left over'. This results in a *contradiction*, unacceptable to traditional logic, but central to Hegelian logic and to Adorno's negative dialectics. The contradiction is, simply put: how can something both *be* and *not be* what it is, at one and the same time? The answer, according to Adorno, is to be found through a critique of traditional rationality and of totalizing systems, with the aim of revealing their ideological content. Applied to music, this leads to a second level of analysis which seeks to reveal the contradictions of the autonomous musical work through situating it in its social and historical context. This approach proceeds by bringing into opposition to the autonomous work that which its apparently self-contained and self-consistent systematization excludes and rejects (or, perhaps more accurately, *represses*): that is, *society*.

(2) At the level of sociological critique Adorno has two basic concerns: (i) to decipher the *social content* of autonomous musical

works; and (ii) to reveal the *social function* of music within the relations of production of capitalist society. The autonomous work, although historically separated from immediate social function, is also at the same time a *fait social* in the Durkheimian sense. As such it takes its place within the social relations of production, and takes on a function (for example, as a commodity within the 'culture industry', consumed as entertainment and subject to fetishization) which may come to oppose the intentionality of the work 'in itself. On the other hand, when the autonomous work is analysed in its own terms, as self-contained object, but with the aim of revealing how society is sedimented in its musical material (in terms of the dialectic between historically and socially situated expressive needs and musical material as handed-down conventions, techniques, technology, etc.), then a certain critical and oppositional tendency may be uncovered. This leads to a contradiction: a work may be 'true' in its own terms – internally consistent with its own 'idea' and intention, critical and self-reflective in relation to its historical tradition – but 'untrue' in terms of its function within the social relations of production. The ideological character of the autonomous work, both 'in itself and in its relation to society, is revealed at this stage its 'untruth' – and this is also an aspect of its truth content.

This further moment of the truth of the work which focuses on *ideology* as uncovered by sociological critique is the falseness of the unity art posits in the face of the evident fragmentation of contemporary society. Thus sociology of music in Adorno's sense involves critique, in that it reveals the ideological moment in autonomous music – how such music also functions as a form of mystification, concealing the repressed contradictions of society and its power relations. Adorno considers, moreover, that music may be regarded as ideological in two senses. On the one hand, music of all kinds may function as ideology in the way in which it is used and marketed: this applies not only to consumer music (that is, popular music), but also to 'great music of the past' like that of

73

Beethoven, initially considered 'an unfolding of truth' in the Hegelian sense but now 'debased by the music business to cultural goods'.[69] On the other hand, autonomous works tend to be ideological *in themselves*, in that, for example, great works of the past, through their harmonious reconcilement of the conflicts set up within the course of the work, give the false appearance of harmony and reconciliation in a real world that is dissonant, fragmented and unreconciled. Thus these first two levels of analysis serve to uncover two conflicting moments of the truth content of the musical work: truth as *consistency* (that which is included), and truth as *ideology* (that which is excluded/repressed). In Hegelian terms these may be taken dialectically as *thesis* and *antithesis*. As such they call for a further level of interpretation, as 'second reflection'. For convenience one may be tempted to take this level as a synthesis of the two previous levels; but it would be wrong to understand this harmonistically, as an attempt to reconcile the irreconcilable. The antagonisms, both within the work and between the work and society, remain. The concern here is evaluation, with the aim of indicating the truth content of the work in relation to the concept of *authenticity*.

(3) The third level, that of philosophical-historical interpretation, contains both the two previous levels of analysis and critique, but maintains that the truth content of works of art cannot be adequately defined simply in terms of consistency or ideology. Philosophical-historical interpretation in this sense seeks to articulate that which in musical works goes beyond the 'facts' of their autonomous technical structure and of their contradictory position and function within social structures. The musical work, as a form of non-conceptual cognition, leaves a 'residue of non-identity' which cannot be subsumed under concepts. Arising out of the tension between mimesis and rationality, between expression and

---

[69] Adorno, 'Ideen zur Musiksoziologie' (1959), in *Klangfiguren: Musikalische Schriften I, Gesammelte Schriften* 16 (Frankfurt am Main: Suhrkamp, 1978), p.10 (my translation).

construction – the dialectic of Subject and Object within the work – is the 'remainder' (*das Mehr*), the riddle of the work. This is related to the problem around which the work is structured as a 'force-field', and which it seeks to solve but which at the same time is also a sign of its failure to solve it. In a sense, Adorno maintains, the work as object inevitably falls short of achieving that to which it aspires. This leaves a paradox which is fundamental to the art work: the riddle itself is insoluble, both in conceptual terms, because it lies beyond concepts, as non-identity, and in art practice, because it lies beyond what it is possible for art to achieve under current social conditions. The aim of Adorno's philosophical interpretation is thus to approach the riddle by identifying the problem of the individual musical work, and by identifying *the reason why* the riddle is insoluble. However, the enigmatic quality of the work is not to be confused with the subjective intention of the composer, nor with the 'Idea' of the composition in the Schoenbergian sense. It seems to exist, as far as one can understand Adorno here, as a kind of after-image, in the gap between what the work achieves in terms of its structure as self-contained object and what it is unable to achieve in terms of reconcilement with society as it is. Although the 'truth' of the work as *consistency* and the 'untruth' of the work as *ideology* are moments of its truth content, in the final analysis it is the *authenticity* of the ways in which the individual work deals with the duality of its position as autonomous object and as social fact which points to its truth; and it is this which calls for philosophical interpretation and evaluation.

From the version of truth content in relation to authenticity, it becomes apparent that the 'truth' of the work for Adorno is not directly identifiable, because it is historically and socially mediated in the work as object. It is the repressed social-historical content of music, and as such needs to be deciphered. The puzzle presented by art works, their sphinx-like appearance, calls for interpretation, for continuation in thought as critique. The need of art works for interpretation is a mark of their inbuilt failure to achieve the sense of all-embracing unity and totality to which they aspire: no matter how self-contained and complete in themselves they may appear, this is an illusion in the face of reality. It is, nevertheless, an illusion which stubbornly refuses to be dispelled, Adorno maintains, even after the disenchantment of the work through analysis, critique and interpretation. The riddle returns to haunt the analyst. In this the enigmatic quality of the work has something of a utopian character which is both implicit in the work and points beyond it, as what Adorno calls the 'necessary illusion' of that which does not exist in the 'false totality' of society as it is. Adorno is not content to allow musical works to remain on the level of 'pure being', nor is he prepared to accept them on the level of simple culinary enjoyment which, he maintains, merely reinforces their commodity character. He is also critical of those forms of art which attempt to break out of art's enforced isolation in the period of modernity through direct intervention in society, in order to make themselves socially or politically useful or relevant (for example, the engagement of Brecht, Eisler and Sartre, and the 'utility' music of composers like Hindemith).[70] He insists that art is to be understood as a form of knowledge, uncompromisingly confronting the problem of its alienation through its relation to its materials. Its 'relevance' arises out of maintaining the potential of the self-reflecting Subject, albeit if only inside that 'enclosed special zone of irrationality within the rationalized world' reserved for art.[71] The history of the development, for example, of high art music in the bourgeois period is one manifestation of the development of the self-reflective expressive Subject as mediated through musical structures. As already discussed, this development is seen from the perspective of the avant garde, from the present stage of the dialectic of the material. The predicament of the historically

[70] See Adorno, 'Commitment', in *The Essential Frankfurt School Reader*, pp.300-18; and 'Gebrauchsmusik' (1924), *Musikalische Schriften VI, Gesammelte Schriften* 19 (Frankfurt am Main: Suhrkamp, 1984), pp.445-7.
[71] Adorno, 'Ideen zur Musiksoziologie', p.14.

and socially defined expressive Subject is immediately that of its relation to its materials – to the system of rules, codes and conventions, the forms, genres and schemata historically changing, as handed down. The hypothesis that this dialectic of the material is mediated by the social dialectic (as 'dialectic of Enlightenment', the process of increasing rationalization of all aspects of social life and the domination of nature) is basic to Adorno's Critical Theory of music. That the goal of this dialectic is the emancipation of the Subject and the freeing of human consciousness from the myth of absolute identity follows from this. Thus the truth content of the work of art hinges on the authenticity of the ways in which the expressive Subject copes with its material in the light of the possibility of freedom, and it is the riddle character of art, its 'magic spell', which seems to keep alive at least the idea of emancipation in what Adorno calls 'the administered world'.

On the one hand it is the process of rationalization that has led to the progressive domination of nature and the elimination of the magical element in art. On the other hand, Adorno proposes that it is precisely through the increasing rationalization of all aspects of the construction of the work of art that art's riddle-character, its 'magic spell', may be preserved. A section from the sixth of his 'Theses upon Art and Religion Today' formulates this paradox and sheds light on what is at the undefined centre of Adorno's critical evaluation of the avant-garde art work in terms of authenticity:

Every work of art still bears the imprint of its magical origin. We may even concede that, if the magical element should be extirpated from art altogether, the decline of art itself will have been reached. This, however, has to be properly understood. First, the surviving magic trends of art are something utterly different from its manifest contents or forms. They are rather to be found in traits, such as the spell cast by any true work of art, the halo of its uniqueness, its inherent claim to represent something absolute. This magic character cannot be conjured up by the desire to keep the flame alive. The actual relationship may

77

be expressed paradoxically. Artistic production cannot escape the universal tendency of Enlightenment – of progressive domination of nature. Throughout the course of history the artist becomes more and more consciously and freely the master of his material and his forms and thus works against the spell of his own product. But it is only his incessant endeavour towards achieving this conscious control and constructive power, only the attack of artistic autonomy on the magic element from which this self-same element draws the strength to survive and to make itself felt in new and more adequate forms. The powers of rational construction brought to bear upon this irrational element seem to increase its inner resistance rather than to eliminate it, as our irrationalist philosophers want to make us believe. Thus the only possible way to save the 'spell' of art is the denial of this spell by art itself. Today it is only the hit composer and best seller writer who prate about the irrationality of their products. Those who create works which are truly concrete and indissoluble, truly antagonistic to the sway of culture industry and calculative manipulation, are those who think most severely and intransigently in terms of technical consistency.[72]

Thus, in plotting this particular constellation of ideas, we arrive at the notion of the truth' of the work as being preserved through uncompromising technical consistency, as negation. The theory is circular, in that it returns us to its starting point – the concrete work as technical structure – while in the process illuminating the complex cross-references linking the work to that which lies outside and beyond itself. Adorno's dialectical method has characteristics of the 'trope' – something noted by Fredric Jameson in his essay 'T.W. Adorno; or, Historical Tropes', where he concludes:

> Yet his concrete studies remain incomparable models of the dialectical process, essays at once both systematic and occasional, in which pretext and consciousness meet to form the most luminous, if

[72] Adorno, 'Theses on Art and Religion Today', in *Noten zur Literatur, Gesammelte Schriften* 11 (Frankfurt am Main: Suhrkamp, 1974), Appendix, p.651 (original in English).

transitory, of figures or tropes of historical intelligibility: 'like its object, knowledge remains shackled to determinate contradiction'.[73]

The Hermeneutic Circle and the Problem of Validation

Adorno's *Aesthetic Theory* is essentially an extended exercise in hermeneutics. The difficulty one is left with, therefore, is the problem common to all hermeneutic theories: that of validation. The relationship between interpretation and the art object is circular, and there is a gap which still remains, in spite of all attempts of interpretation to bridge it through drawing on shared traditions and particular theories of society and history. Within the hermeneutic circle there are no absolute interpretations, the truth of which can be logically demonstrated in any positivist sense. Thus the 'illuminations' thrown up by Adorno's dialectical hermeneutics can easily be seen as mere speculation and opinion, and there is nothing in the interpretation of Adorno offered in this essay caught as it is within the same circle – which is able to refute such a view. All that I have been able to do here is to clarify the theoretical framework and system of values within which Adorno works, and to make explicit his dialectical method and the levels of analysis, critique and interpretation between which, I argue, he shifts. And even if I had set out to ground the generality of his theory in the particularity of individual works, in terms of, for example, Adorno's own technical music analyses (of which there are many, especially of works by Schoenberg, Berg and Webern[74]),

---

[73] Fredric Jameson, 'T. W. Adorno; or, Historical Tropes', in *Marxism and Form* (Princeton: Princeton University, 1971), p.59 (reference to Adorno, *Philosophy of Modern Music*, p.33).

[74] For Adorno's 'Interpretationsanalysen' of individual works by Webern and Berg, see *Der getreue Korrepetitor, Gesammelte Schriften* 15 (Frankfurt/Main: Suhrkamp, 1976); of works by Berg, see *Berg: Der Meister des kleinsten Übergangs, Gesammelte Schriften* 13 (Frankfurt/Main: Suhrkamp, 1971); of works by Schoenberg, see *Musikalische Schriften V, Gesammelte Schriften* 18 (Frankfurt/Main: Suhrkamp, 1984).

it is unlikely that anything approaching empirical verification of his claims on the level of philosophical interpretation could have been achieved. The reason for this, I suggest, does not lie in the inadequacy of his rather traditional motivic-thematic technical analyses (different as they are from the kind of 'hermeneutic' analysis practised in books like *Philosophy of New Music*[75] and *Versuch über Wagner*[76]); neither does it really lie in the absence of any firm empirical basis for his philosophical interpretations. The failure of Adorno to break out of the hermeneutic circle and to bridge the gap between analysis and interpretation points instead to a fundamental problem of music analysis itself. Perhaps his most valuable contribution to music theory has been to focus on this dilemma: that is, the problem which faces technical analysis when it tries to move beyond the closed circle of the work and involve itself in anything more than what Adorno has called 'humanistic stocktaking'. His project serves to reveal the limits of empiricism and positivism faced with the persistent enigma of the art work in relation to its 'social other'.

[75] Adorno later became critical of the approach he had taken in *Philosophy of New Music* 'because the book did not obey its own principle as strictly as it was dutybound to do' (Über das gegenwärtige Verhältnis von Philosophie und Musik' [1953], *Musikalische Schriften V, Gesammelte Schriften* 18, p.165). He is referring to his principle that the philosophical interpretation of music should always proceed from the experience and analysis of individual works, whereas *Philosophy of New Music* had tended to deal with 'the material as such and its movement through abstraction, . . . independently of its crystallization in the works themselves' (ibid., my translation). He considers that this may have given the false impression that music could be totally subsumed under concepts.

[76] Adorno, *Versuch über Wagner* (1952), *Gesammelte Schriften* 13; translated by Rodney Livingstone as *In Search of Wagner* (London: NLB, 1981); Marc Jiminez criticizes Adorno's Wagner book for focusing on the composer's identity and personality, because this results in an a priori judgment on the music itself. He contrasts this with the approach taken in *Philosophy of New Music*, which starts instead from an examination of the compositional procedures of the two composers on which it focuses (see Jiminez, *Adorno: art, idéologie et théorie de l'art*, Paris: Union Générale d'Éditions, 1973, pp.60-1).

3 Adorno, Popular Music and Mass Culture[1]

Adorno's critique of popular music is generally considered the least convincing aspect of his analysis of the predicament of Western music in the twentieth century. The immediate reasons as to why his views on popular music are difficult to accept are obvious enough, and it must be admitted that the usual criticisms that Adorno is prejudiced, arrogant and uninformed in this field contain more than a grain of truth. However, my intention here is not to add anything new by way of invective, nor is it to attack Adorno's basic thesis regarding the dilemma facing twentieth-century culture as a whole. Instead, I propose to offer some suggestions as to how Adorno's writings on popular music may be approached so that the end result is something more than outright dismissal of his extreme and often dogmatic value judgments. It is an attempt to rescue the baby from the bath water, so to speak, as it seems to me that hidden in his theory there remains a potential which was never properly recognized by Adorno.

[1] This essay is a slightly modified version of an article which originally appeared in *Popular Music 2: Theory and Method*, eds. Richard Middleton and David Horn (Cambridge: Cambridge University Press, 1982), pp.201-18. I am grateful to the publishers for allowing me to republish it here.

Two points, however, need to be emphasized from the outset: first, that Adorno's critique of popular music is only to be understood in relation to his analysis of the predicament of 'serious music' in the twentieth century; and second, that positive solutions and straightforward answers are not to be expected. As everyone who has attempted to read Adorno's complex and maddening prose quickly discovers, it does not offer answers, but contradictions, formulated with such extreme density that they become inescapable.

My argument is that, in order to avoid the polarized 'either/or' type of judgment which inevitably arises here, Adorno's own views have to be subjected to his own medicine – that is, to his own 'negative dialectics'. As I hope will become clear, his work actually demands and provokes this kind of dialectical approach in order to be understood at all. This involves reminding ourselves of his methodology, as well as looking at his theory of mass culture *per se*. Only after doing this are we really in a position to criticize his ideas constructively and discover whether his own subjective prejudices and blind spots are actually the fatal flaws they are usually seen to be in connection with his theories on popular music. Finally, it is interesting to see what is left over after his ideas have been subjected to such treatment: anything which – however paradoxical it remains – may still be relevant to the ways in which jazz and rock music have developed since the 1950s and 1960s.

1. Contradiction as Method

The main difficulty in reading Adorno (and this applies, of course, not only to the writings on popular music) is that the texts themselves, because of their extreme complexity and the exaggerated nature of the views expressed, tend to arouse a great deal of irritation and resistance in the reader. As a consequence it is very easy to lose sight of the separate strands of Adorno's arguments and the broader context of ideas to which his thought refers at every point. All that then remains is a succession of provocative overstatements, apparently contradicting one another, and each one unacceptable as it stands. The result of this kind of fragmented reading is, to say the least, misunderstanding: for, although Adorno's approach is essentially anti-systematic and fragmentary, it also has underlying it what can, with justification, be called a 'methodology'. For this reason, therefore, and in order to counteract the tendency to become fixated on the individual (and exaggerated) elements which make up his argument, it is important that Adorno be read in the light of his own method, while at every point (and he is constantly changing perspective) the connection has also to be made with the context of his theory as a whole. Hence the amount of space I shall devote to providing such a context, before proceeding to the criticisms and suggestions contained in sections 3 and 4.

What, then, is Adorno's method? It is useful to consider an example here which can also serve as a point of reference for much of what follows. It is taken from the early essay 'On the Social Situation of Music' ('Zur gesellschaftlichen Lage der Musik'), which Adorno published in the *Zeitschrift für Sozialforschung* in 1932, but never subsequently allowed to be reprinted:

> There is no longer any 'folk' left whose songs and games could be taken up and sublimated by art. The opening up of the markets together with the effect of the bourgeois rationalization process have put the whole of society–even ideologically – under bourgeois categories, and the categories of contemporary vulgar music are altogether those of bourgeois rationalized society, which, in order to remain consumable, are kept only to within the limits of awareness which bourgeois society imposes on the oppressed classes as well as on itself. The material used by vulgar music is the obsolete and degenerated material of art music.[2]

[2] Adorno, 'Zur gesellschaftlichen Lage der Musik', *Zeitschrift für Sozialforschung*, I (1932), p.373 (my trans.).

As formulated, this is distinctly provocative. What is meant here by 'vulgar music', and by the notion that 'the material used by vulgar music is the obsolete and degenerated material of art music' will be considered later. What I wish to concentrate on for the moment is Adorno's typical method of procedure: that is to say, contradiction and exaggeration as method – the revealing of a fundamental contradiction, and the formulation of its opposite poles by means of exaggeration. Examples of this are to be found on practically every page Adorno wrote. The progression is always tripartite: (i) the dilemma is uncompromisingly stated (Sentence I); (ii) the tension between the poles ('folk' (vulgar music)/art) leads to what could almost be seen as a kind of synthesis, in the best Hegelian manner (although Adorno would regard it more as an 'illumination' of the implications of the initial statement) (Sentence II); (iii) finally comes the reformulation of the initial dilemma, now inverted, and even more uncompromisingly stated than ever (Sentence III). Although revealed, the terms of the contradiction remain unreconciled.

The process is dialectical in that, although diametrically opposed, the two poles of the contradiction are at the same time intimately related, as two sides of the same basic phenomenon. Adorno warns us, however, that the dialectical method is by no means merely 'the serene demonstration of the fact that there are two sides to everything'.[3] Adorno's formulations always have a quite deliberate irritation value. His intention is not to restore an illusory equilibrium, wherein all tension (what he calls the force-field) between the extremes is conveniently neutralized. Hence his calculated use of exaggeration. The approach is also negative in that it is basically critical; positive solutions or alternatives are not offered. The contradictions as Adorno formulates them are unacceptable, and active participation is

[3] Adorno, *Minima Moralia* (1951), trans. E.F.N. Jephcott (London: Verso, 1974), p.247.

demanded from the reader, left dangling on the horns of the dilemma.

But although on the one hand Adorno is aiming to provoke the reader into self-reflection, it has at the same time to be stressed that he also conceives the contradictions as being immanent to the object of investigation. That is to say that music, as object, already contains social contradictions within itself, within its actual material structure. The development of tonal structures in Western music, and the subsequent breakdown of those structures and the ensuing fragmentation of musical language in the twentieth century, are regarded by Adorno as a reflection and indeed manifestation of the tendencies of bourgeois culture/society itself. For Adorno, therefore, it is a question of uncovering the contradictions (hidden as they are in what, for us, has now become 'second nature'), and deciphering their significance within the context of society and culture as a whole. And he maintains, furthermore, that it is only in their most extreme formulation that the significance of the contradictions may be revealed. He is not interested in trying to catalogue and explain all the various degrees that lie between the extremes. He goes instead straight for the extremes themselves, insisting that it is in the light of the tension between its opposite poles that the 'whole' becomes intelligible. The poles represent the extreme tendencies of the individual parts within the context of the whole, and exaggeration may thus be seen as the stylistic device employed to highlight these tendencies and to bring them vividly into consciousness. Quite apart from its well-known indebtedness to Hegelian-Marxian dialectics, the approach derives much from Freud; in *Minima Moralia* Adorno wrote (with characteristic exaggeration): 'In psychoanalysis nothing is true except the exaggerations'.[4]

[4] Ibid., p.49.

2. Theory of Mass Culture

Adorno's method operates within the context of a theory which regards 'serious' and 'popular' music as potentially forming two complementary halves of one whole – although we may be forgiven for not immediately recognizing this in certain of his articles (like those, for example, on jazz). For him the split is not essentially between serious and popular as such – a division which has become, in his view, increasingly meaningless due to the effect of the culture industry and the almost inescapable commodity character of all cultural products in the twentieth century. The split is much more that between, on the one hand, music which accepts its character as commodity, thus becoming identical with the machinations of the culture industry itself, and, on the other hand, a self-reflective music which critically opposes its fate as commodity, and thus ends up by alienating itself from society by becoming unacceptable to it. As Gillian Rose puts it in her book on Adorno:

> Adorno examined the 'contradiction between the forces and the relations of production'. His analyses of every kind of music (were) based on the premise that commodity fetishism (reification) in music had increased, that the commodity character of music was deeply affected by the new modes of mechanical reproduction and the new possibilities of exchange and distribution... The 'contradiction' occurs between those kinds of music which adapt to the prevalent modes of exchange and reception and music which resists them, and also within the latter kind of music. Under the relations of production Adorno looks at music which adapts, and under forces of production he looks at music which resists adaptation.[5]

As far as Adorno is concerned, therefore, the fundamental contradiction is now between these two kinds of music. For

[5] Gillian Rose, *The Melancholy Science*, pp.131-2.

convenience I shall refer to them from now on as category one and category two.

Music of category one – the uncritical and unreflective type – has an 'objective' character, in that it has become identical with the collective tendencies of society itself, which it affirms and automatically reflects. It is, according to Adorno, an affirmation of the situation as it is ('mere existence', as he often calls it, sustained by what he terms 'identity thinking'). Total identification with 'that which is' – the established order – means, Adorno maintains, the total exclusion of all that does not fit conveniently into that order. And it is, he insists, precisely in the direction of that which does not fit, of that which is ignored, disdained or excluded, where that which is true is still to be glimpsed.

For Adorno, art (and indeed society itself) must seek to become conscious of and to integrate that which previously had been neglected by established structures. But in so doing the structures themselves are compelled to change radically. The process is thus a dynamic one which, of its very nature, is critically opposed to static and established systems, although at the same time it is still to a considerable extent dependent upon traditional structures for its material. It is precisely the stifling of this process, and the total identification with regressive and obsolete aspects of traditional structures, which characterize the uncritical music of category one. Such 'false consciousness' and 'identity thinking' are epitomized by the commodity form, and the music of category one, Adorno maintains, has acquired the fetish character of the commodity and has become reified. To put it in Marxian terms: its value in exchange – its marketability – is reified into an objective characteristic of the commodity itself. Music acts as a kind of 'social cement', wherein the individual sacrifices his individuality to the totality. All significance becomes invested in music as an object of exchange, focusing on what Adorno regards as non-essential and secondary features at the expense of any understanding of the whole. As he puts it: 'the moments of sensual pleasure in the idea, the voice, the instrument are made into fetishes and torn away from any functions which would give them meaning'.[6] These tendencies in the production and distribution (or composition and reproduction) stages also have their counterpart at the reception stage, in what Adorno calls the regression of listening. This manifests itself in an atomized and passive form of musical experience – a kind of theme-tune listening – which only registers isolated musical events: for example, easily memorable melodic fragments, striking instrumental colour, repetitive rhythms, etc. There is a constant demand for the familiar and easily recognizable, and such a mode of listening is actually encouraged by the culture industry; indeed it is built into the structure of popular music itself to produce a situation where 'the composition listens for the listener'.[7] This feature of popular music Adorno calls standardization: a piece is totally made up of easily recognizable and (through frequent repetition) generally accepted formulae, within an overall scheme which remains always basically the same. Between the individual details that make up the piece and its form there is no interaction, and the primary result of this is that 'the listener becomes prone to evince stronger reactions to the part than to the whole'.[8] And in the article 'On Popular Music' he writes: 'the whole is pre-given and preaccepted, even before the actual experience of the music starts'.[9]

Although, in connection with standardization, Adorno is specifically referring to what he conceives as popular music, his first category – that of 'uncritical' music – actually encompasses all music which is unable to resist exploitation as commodity,

[6] Adorno, 'On the Fetish Character in Music and the Regression of Listening' (1938), trans. anon., in *The Essential Frankfurt School Reader*, ed. A. Arato and E. Gebhardt (Oxford: Basil Blackwell, 1978), p.277.

[7] Ibid, p.290.

[8] Adorno, *Introduction to the Sociology of Music* (1962), trans. E.B. Ashton (New York: Seabury Press,1976), p.29.

[9] Adorno, 'On Popular Music' (with George Simpson), *Studies in Philosophy and Social Sciences* 9 (1941), p.18.

however unwittingly. It includes not only popular music, but also serious music of the past, now reduced to the level of museum exhibits or mere entertainment, as well as that 'modern' music which attempts some form of compromise for the sake of accessibility.

The second category – that of critical, self-reflective music – has, according to Adorno, a 'subjective' character, in that it opposes the situation as it is and strives, through negation, to retain a necessary tension between Subject and Object, individual and collectivity. It thus attempts to reveal cracks in the 'false totality' through which that which is 'not yet identical' may still be glimpsed. However, such music dare not affirm this 'glimpse of truth', because such an affirmation would immediately deliver it up again to the culture industry. Hence the paradox of what for Adorno constitutes authentic music in the twentieth century: it is compelled to deny meaning in order to preserve it. While, in previous, different historical conditions, authentic music had been able to contain a strong affirmative element as counterbalance to its negative, critical function (Adorno cites the example of Beethoven), authentic music is now, in Adorno's view, essentially that of the serious avant garde. It is a non-standardized, radical music, which formulates its self-reflection' within its actual compositional structure (although what this means in practical terms is not always clear). In so doing, it not only reflects the tendencies of society by passively mirroring them (as, Adorno maintains, does popular music) but simultaneously and actively opposes these tendencies by its negation of standardized meaning within its own structure. Thus the 'meaning' of such music is this very negation of accepted meanings. And, at the reception stage, such music demands what Adorno calls 'structural listening' – a form of listening whereby the listener hears the parts in relation to the whole, and is able to recognize the unfolding of the objective significance of the work over against his/her own subjective demands and associations.

Although it should be stressed that Adorno himself would probably not have wished to present the above two categories as systematically as I have attempted to do here, the contrast between them nevertheless does serve to highlight a number of his most important concepts. As a pair of opposites these concepts pinpoint aspects of the basic contradiction which Adorno manages to reveal in everything he examines: namely, that in the twentieth century the essential and creative relationship between Subject and Object, individual and collectivity, negation and affirmation, non–identity and identity, part and whole, has broken down. The precarious autonomy of the self-reflecting individual, as Subject, is in danger of succumbing completely to the 'objective' demands of the totality. 'The liquidation of the individual is the real signature of the new musical situation', as he puts it.[10]

So far the intention has been to provide a methodological and theoretical framework. It is not the broad outlines of this framework that I now intend to criticize, but rather certain specific aspects of the critique of popular music which I regard as being inconsistent with Adorno's theory as a whole.

3. The Critique Criticized

Although, as we have seen, Adorno considers the main split to be that between 'uncritical' and 'critical', or 'standardized' and 'non-standardized' music, he also, of course, leaves us in no doubt as to which of the two categories popular music belongs. It does not seriously seem to have occurred to him that certain kinds of popular music may also at times be able to meet his requirements for the music of category two, and contain a moment of genuine protest. As far as he is concerned, popular music is indistinguishable from the culture industry itself, its purpose being that of

[10] Adorno, 'On the Fetish Character in Music and the Regression of Listening', p.276.

entertainment and distraction (Adorno seemed unable to recognize that music may also quite validly perform a recreational function). And furthermore, he maintains, the pleasure promised by popular music is illusory, as with all commodities, and 'is given only to be denied'.[11] As he puts it: 'it occupies the pockets of silence that develop between people moulded by anxiety, work and undemanding docility'.[12]

But what does he really mean when he says 'popular music'? It is certainly a blanket term as he uses it. The terms 'popular' (or vulgar) music and *leichte Musik* – usually applied remarkably indiscriminately – seem to account conveniently for practically everything that is not serious music. Wolfgang Sandner, in his article 'Popularmusik als somatisches Stimulans', points out that Adorno's 'devastating verdict on so-called popular music has probably not been relativized up to now because at least one of these forms of popular music (and quantitatively the largest at that) can well be regarded as justifying his judgment'.[13] It is, of course, the commercial hit song that he means here. But what of the other forms?

As Sandner shows, when Adorno's concept of popular music is examined, it disintegrates into a multiplicity of different elements, among which may be distinguished, for example, light music, hit tunes, dance music, jazz and folk music. Such lack of differentiation is quite astonishing in someone who, in the area of serious music, is normally so insistent on the necessity for making the most subtle distinctions. The explanation which most readily springs to mind – and it is no explanation at all – is that Adorno simply detested popular music, and in assessing it was content to give way to his own irrational prejudices in the most uncritical and

[11] Ibid. p.271.

[12] Ibid. p.271.

[13] Wolfgang Sandner, 'Popularmusik als somatisches Stimulans: Adornos Kritik der "leichten Musik"', in *Adorno und die Musik*, ed. Otto Kolleritsch (Graz: Universal Edition,1973), p.125 (my trans.).

unreflective manner. If so, then such a reaction certainly constitutes a blind spot which needs closer examination. Indeed, as
Adorno himself has pointed out in connection with his 'psycho'-
analyses of serious music, it is precisely the 'blotches' that are of
most significance – the unintentional and unconscious flaws. This
approach can just as profitably be turned back on to Adorno
himself to try to account for some of his own more striking
inconsistencies.

It is revealing to look at Adorno's judgment on popular music
within the context of the historical period from which the concept
of the 'culture industry' and Critical Theory itself emerged: that
is, the late 1920s, the 1930s and the early 1940s. This period saw
the refinement of techniques of mechanical reproduction, the
development of radio and of the sound film, and the increasing
power of the mass media with all the opportunities offered for
ideological exploitation. The same period also saw the rise of the
European dictatorships and the degeneration of culture brought
about by the proliferation of totalitarian regimes. These were the
formative years in Adorno's own development. By the time he
returned to Germany in the late 1940s, after his exile in America,
his theories – particularly on popular culture and ideology had
reached their final form. It is to this period – the 1930s and early
1940s – that Adorno's definitive writings on the culture industry
and popular music belong: 'On the Social Situation of Music'
(1932); 'On Jazz' (1936); 'On the Fetish Character in Music and
the Regression of Listening' (1938); and the article written in
English (with George Simpson) called 'On Popular Music' (1941).
Against this historical background it is not difficult to understand
the extreme importance Adorno attached to the necessity for
revealing the levels at which ideology operates within art. It is also
within this context that hints can be found which go some way
towards explaining Adorno's dogmatic and inflexible attitude
towards popular music. Wolfgang Sandner has asked the obvious
but crucial question: just what was the all-pervading mass music of

this period, particularly in the late 1920s and early 1930s in both Western Europe and America, which Adorno would have found inescapable every time he turned on the radio?

As becomes clear, what Adorno so curiously labelled 'jazz', and what he was ever after to denigrate as empty mannerism, ephemeral fashion, 'light music . . . dressed up' with frills (as he wrote in an article in 1953, 'Perennial Fashion – Jazz'),[14] was in fact the music of the dance band craze so much a feature of the time, and epitomized by the slick arrangements of Paul Whiteman and his band. This music, although it derives its store of effects from authentic jazz' in terms of danceable rhythms and characteristic instrumental sound, is essentially commercialized mass music and, as such, is hardly what would be associated with the term 'jazz' today. Sandner concludes, therefore, that when Adorno says 'jazz', it is not actually jazz that he means, but the jazz-influenced dance music of the 1920s and early 1930s. The confusion can be to some extent justified in Adorno's case, in that it was during this period that jazz became particularly identified with commercialized dance music and hit songs, and achieved a commercial success that it had not enjoyed previously nor has it enjoyed since. Seen in the context of the period, therefore, Adorno's judgments become more understandable and, to an extent, valid.

But the intention here is not simply to justify Adorno's misunderstandings. The fact is that, in putting Adorno's critique of popular music (and in particular of what he calls 'jazz') into its historical perspective, a number of other questions are immediately raised. Why, for instance – even allowing for the possible validity of his critique in the context of the commercial music of the 1930s and early 1940s – did he never allow for the possibility that popular music in certain of its manifestations might be able to change its function? And why did he never afterwards make an

---

[14] Adorno, 'Perennial Fashion – Jazz' (1953), in *Prisms* (1955), trans. Samuel and Shierry Weber (London: Neville Spearman, 1967), pp.122-3.

effort to become better acquainted with current developments in jazz (and later, rock music) in order at least to check if his theories still fitted? Adorno lived right through the 1960s (he died in 1969) and could hardly have been unaware of the role played by the new rock music and jazz in the hippy and student movements.

In attempting to answer such questions it is difficult not to agree with Sandner's suggestion that Adorno had simply 'absolutized' his image of jazz and of the 'impotent jazz subject' as he had developed it in the 1930s, and never afterwards modified it because he never again took the trouble to listen to such music. As Sandner puts it: 'In 1936 Adorno gave up giving jazz any real thought (without, however, giving up writing about it) – and this at a time when this music first began to free itself from the historically determined functions which bound it to the sphere of "amusement" '.[15] In 'Perennial Fashion – Jazz', for example, written in the 1950s, Adorno demonstrates, if anything, a hardening of his earlier views.

But what of so-called 'light music'? Here Adorno allows himself to be more indulgent in what he has to say. Although the spheres of light (or popular music – the terms still seems largely interchangeable as far as he is concerned) and serious music are now separated, they had previously been much closer, and had interacted to their mutual benefit. For Adorno, the ultimate synthesis of serious and popular occurred in Mozart's *The Magic Flute*, after which, he writes, 'it was never again possible to force serious and light music together'.[16] But even in the nineteenth century, light music still apparently had something to offer in relation to serious music, and accordingly the operettas of Offenbach, the waltzes of Strauss and Viennese operetta are treated by Adorno with a kind of paternal tolerance. Light music is regarded as a kind of pendant to serious music – an immature and possibly rather frivolous poor

[15] Sandner, 'Popularmusik als somatisches Stimulans', p.129 (my trans.).
[16] Adorno, 'On the Fetish Character in Music and the Regression of Listening', p.273.

relation, but nevertheless not to be totally dismissed merely on that account, as after all it is still one of the family.[17] Historically, serious or 'high art' music had renewed its lost strength by borrowing from time to time from the 'lower', from 'vulgar' music (and here light music seems to tail off into folk music). Now, however, it is the lower which plays with the scraps which have fallen from the table of the higher music. That is, in the increasing split which has developed between the two spheres, Adorno maintains, as we have seen, that the lower music becomes merely the degenerated form of what the higher was at a previous stage.

As far as folk music is concerned, Adorno is relatively noncommittal (apart from commenting that, as noted, 'there is no longer any "folk" left' anyway). His indifference to folk music, and to the music of cultures outside the tradition of western music, can well be regarded as yet another manifestation of his absorption in what are essentially German cultural values. He does acknowledge, however, the importance of the influence of folk music on composers like Janáček and Bartók, but points out that here the peasant music of agrarian southeast Europe had escaped the effects of the culture industry and was therefore able in its turn, at a particular historical moment, to have a vital and significant effect upon the tradition of European art music itself.[18] This almost seems to constitute an exception to Adorno's theory as a whole – until, however, it is remembered that the theory is essentially a critique of the industrialized culture of the West at what he calls 'the most advanced stage of its historical dialectic', and this also applies, of course, to the historical dialectic of the musical material itself. The theory is only peripherally (if at all) concerned with the industrially less-developed societies of the East. Nevertheless, an unexpected loophole does present itself here, and one which may still yet be relevant to the interaction between serious and popular

[17] See Sandner, 'Popularmusik als somatisches Stimulans', p.129.
[18] Adorno, *Philosophy of Modern Music*, p.3 Note.

95

(in this case folk) music – that is, if it is at all conceivable that so-called folk and ethnic musics are still able to withstand the all-pervading effects of the culture industry in the late twentieth century.

It is now interesting to return to jazz and hit songs (and ultimately rock music) within the context of our consideration of light music and folk music, as there is one final assumption of Adorno's which still needs to be questioned: the assumption that 'the material used by vulgar music is the obsolete and degenerated material of art music'. This seems a valid enough formulation as far as light music and commercial hit songs are concerned (at least, with the definitions I have attempted to assign them here). But is it valid for jazz – at least for that 'authentic' jazz to which Adorno seems to have been determined to turn a deaf ear? It may well be argued that the African roots of jazz have at times been over-emphasized, but Adorno goes to the other extreme and tries to deny any importance to the non-European influence on this music. In so doing he condemns it to the lowest possible stage in the degeneration and disintegration of the material of Western serious music itself. It is apparently not only regarded as a degeneration of the material of serious music, but even as being a degeneration of the material of light music and of the commercial hit song. It also seems safe to assume that it is to somewhere within these nether regions that Adorno would have allotted rock music – had he bothered to listen to it.

Ironically, it is the very polarity between jazz and rock music on the one hand and 'avant-garde' and 'experimental' music on the other which seems to have given rise to a change of function in the 'lower' towards the direction of 'serious' art. This is a change of function which Adorno himself would doubtless have found hard to accept, even though the implications of his own theory certainly allow for it.

4. Popular Music and Critical Self-Reflection

In the course of the above criticisms I have frequently referred to Wolfgang Sandner's article, 'Popularmusik als somatisches Stimulans'. I shall now expand on a number of the points he raises. At the same time, however, I find it necessary to go one step beyond what I consider to be Sandner's rather excessive optimism. The argument has ultimately to be brought full circle, as, in spite of all, Adorno's 'paradox' cannot be disposed of so easily. But first I should like to examine the implications hidden in Adorno's theory in more depth.

As has been shown, there is a disturbing lack of differentiation to be seen at many points in Adorno's critique of popular music – something which tends, in fact, to give his work in this area the kind of authoritarian undertones he was always so quick to reveal in others. This has certainly hindered a more general acceptance of his ideas on popular music. But these undeniable flaws should not blind us to the potential contained in the theory as a whole to transcend the personal blind spots which are apparent in his application of the theory to the particular case of so-called popular music. As we have seen, Adorno did not pursue the implications of his critique with his usual stringency because he was quite simply prevented from doing so by his own reified concepts, bound as they were to the dance music and hit tunes of the 1930s. In order to reveal the critique's hidden potential for popular music, we must turn once more to Adorno's writings on serious art. In keeping with the argument presented in the following extracts, the points raised here have themselves largely escaped the notice of most of his commentators and critics. In *Minima Moralia* there occurs the following passage:

> If Benjamin said [Benjamin 1970, pp. 258-9] that history had hitherto been written from the standpoint of the victor, and needed to be written from that of the vanquished, we might add that knowledge must indeed present the fatally rectilinear succession of victory and

defeat, but should also address itself to those things which were not embraced by this dynamic, which fell by the wayside – what might be called the waste products and blind spots that have escaped the dialectic. It is in the nature of the defeated to appear, in their impotence, irrelevant, eccentric, derisory. What transcends the ruling society is not only the potentiality it develops but also all that which did not fit properly into the laws of historical movement. Theory must needs deal with cross-grained, opaque, unassimilated material, which as such admittedly has from the start an anachronistic quality, but is not wholly obsolete since it has outwitted the historical dynamic. This can most readily be seen in art.[19]

From this it becomes clear that Adorno allows for the possibility of a music which can exist meaningfully outside the historical dialectic and the dominant system itself – or rather, which exists within that system but which escapes being embraced by it. It belongs to neither of the two extreme tendencies within twentieth-century serious music as presented by Adorno in *Philosophy of New Music*. It is therefore neither the music of a Schoenberg, which attempts to develop and rationalize the tendencies and contradictions of the traditional tonal system *from within* so that they turn back on themselves and reflect themselves, nor is it the music of a Stravinsky which, according to Adorno, attempts to reconcile the contradictions *from the outside* by resorting, for example, to stylistic forms of the past. It lies, instead, somewhere between the two extremes. For its material it draws on the left-overs and worn-out gestures of traditional (mainly nineteenth-century) music as well as the stock formulae of popular (that is, consumer) music, but gives them new meaning by putting them in an entirely new context. The contradictions of the material are both revealed and held unreconciled within the compositional structure. Such music is therefore regarded by Adorno as critical and self-reflective, and it thus comes under his concept of 'authentic' music.

[19] Adorno, *Minima Moralia*, p.151.

It is significant to follow up this line of thought with reference to three further examples taken from Adorno's writings. First, the unique case of Erik Satie; in *Minima Moralia* Adorno writes: 'in Satie's pert and puerile piano pieces there are flashes of experience undreamed of by the school of Schoenberg, with all its rigour and all the pathos of musical development behind it'.[20] But in a certain sense even Satie's art stands outside the type we are attempting to describe here, since according to Adorno it has much in common with children's art, in that it is neither progressive nor regressive, neither opposes the dominant system nor identifies with it, but simply declines it.[21] The second example – Gustav Mahler – more clearly fits Adorno's requirements:

> It is not for nothing that Mahler is the scandal of all bourgeois musical ethics. They call him uncreative because he suspends their concept of creation itself. Everything with which he occupies himself is already there. He accepts it in its vulgarised form; his themes are expropriated ones. Nevertheless, nothing sounds as it was wont to; all things are diverted as if by a magnet. What is worn out yields pliantly to the improvising hand; the used parts win a second life as variants.[22]

And in our third example – the music Kurt Weill wrote in collaboration with Brecht – Adorno is more explicit still. As early as 1932 he writes that Weill's music of this period belongs to a type which 'refuses positive solutions and contents itself with revealing the cracks in the social totality . . . without giving them the benefit (of the illusion) of aesthetic totality. For this it avails itself partly of the style of expression of nineteenth-century bourgeois music

---

[20] Ibid., p.151.

[21] Ibid.

[22] Adorno, 'On the Fetish Character in Music and the Regression of Listening', p.298.

culture and partly of present-day consumer music'.[23] And further, Weill's style is

> a montage-style, which negates and at the same time raises to a new level [*aufhebt*] the surface appearance of neo-classicism and juxtaposes and cements ruins and fragments up against one another [*aneinander rückt*] through the addition of 'wrong notes', it composes out the falseness and pretence which today have become apparent in the harmonic language of the nineteenth century.[24]

These examples are sufficient to establish that Adorno had recognized the possibility of working meaningfully with regressive tonal and formal material – within the sphere of serious music, that is. It now merely remains to consider whether the same possibility also exists within the sphere of popular music – and, if so, to ask what are the implications of this in terms of Adorno's theory?

To return for a moment to the notion that the material used by popular music is the material of serious music, now become obsolete: Adorno seemed to find it inconceivable that this process could also, in a certain sense, operate the other way round. But, as Sandner points out, 'in the history of both jazz and rock music there is quite clearly to be seen an almost obsessive pressure from the "sub-culture" towards "high art" music'.[25] This 'pressure' can be understood as being symptomatic of the increasing degree of self-reflection within certain kinds of more radical popular music. In becoming increasingly aware of its function and of the nature of its own material (in terms of the stock formulae of rock music, ballads, etc., as well as developments in studio techniques, new technology and the synthesis and manipulation of sound), and also in drawing increasingly on the material and techniques of twentieth-century art music, radical popular music has tended to take on a critical character and to manifest this not only in the

[23] Adorno, 'Zur gesellschaftlichen Lage der Musik', p.108 (my trans.).

[24] Ibid., p.122.

[25] Sandner, 'Popularmusik als somatisches Stimulans', p.130 (my trans.).

texts of the songs, but also within the construction of the music itself. This is apparent in the work of certain rock bands of the 1960s and 1970s. The obvious example is Frank Zappa. In mirroring contemporary culture – from Sinatra to Varèse – as a giant scrap heap of disposable consumer trash, Zappa must certainly come as close as any to meeting Adorno's requirements as outlined in the above extract on Weill. With Zappa it is not only that his music reflects contemporary American reality, but that it does this with such imagination, intelligence and irony and with such awareness of the extraordinary variety of material and techniques at his disposal. Frank Zappa is, of course, only one example of this tendency. Many others, in both rock music and jazz, could equally well be cited: The Velvet Underground – especially on records like *White Light/White Heat* inevitably come to mind here, as do the solo albums John Cale made after he left the group. Another example is Carla Bley's *Escalator over the Hill*, while in Britain such groups as Henry Cow and The Art Bears have been notable for their uncompromisingly experimental stance, not to mention some post-punk bands. To be at all comprehensive a list like this would need to include musicians and groups working in the general area of avant-garde rock and jazz in France, Italy, Germany, Holland and Scandinavia as well as in America and Britain. But the main point being made here is that a marked feature of certain kinds of jazz and – in particular – rock music since the 1960s is the demand to be taken seriously, the compulsion towards the condition of the serious avant garde, manifested in the degree of self-examination going on within the music itself. This is a state of affairs which inevitably carries with it its own in-built conflict – its own 'immanent contradiction', as Adorno would have put it. Before finally turning to consider this particular contradiction, however, I want first to look at a few things Adorno had to say about the nature of musical self-reflection in general.

In his essay 'Music and technique' of 1959 Adorno has

suggested that hope lies, if anywhere, in the continuing dialectic between music and technique. Technique, he insists, is no longer something external to the 'inner meaning' of the work. It is not merely the objective aspect of the work through which its subject-ive, 'spiritual' inner meaning is mediated. Technique has now penetrated to the heart of the work itself, and 'the interior and exterior produce each other alternatingly and mutually'.[26] With the increasing 'technification' of music, technique – particularly in terms of technical reproduction – becomes increasingly incorpor-ated into the actual production/composition of music itself. This is something that may be taken as applying especially to contem-porary popular music, in its obsession with sound and the modifi-cation of sound.[27] The danger, as Adorno sees it (in connection with serious music), lies in the swamping of the subjective element by its total 'technification'. But the chance of a way out, he main-tains, lies in a critical, self-reflective attitude towards this process within the structure of the music itself.

> The progressive intertwining of art and technique is not necessarily to be accepted as irrevocable; indeed, it contains the potential of a more positive development. . . . Perhaps help lies only in ruthless reflection of the process upon itself, a technical examination of technique even in those instances where it offers itself to the self-critical ear as a wall without either cracks or handholds. If the time has really come for music to turn once again to the subject, then this must not be done in such a way that the intention is again immersed only in the subject. Mediation through the subject can succeed only in objective terms, as criticism of the technical context in itself – not of those things which one might think or feel, not even of that which one might hear imaginatively in isolated inwardness.[28]

---

[26] Adorno, 'Music and Technique' (1958), trans. Wesley Blomster, *Telos* 32 (1977), p.80.

[27] Cf. Sandner, 'Popularmusik als somatisches Stimulans', p.130.

[28] Adorno, 'Music and Technique', p.88.

Although obviously it is serious music that is being referred to here, there appears to be no reason why Adorno's argument should not apply just as well to the kind of radical popular music we have just been considering. However, if Adorno's critique does allow, in spite of itself, for the possibility of a critical popular music which aspires towards our category two, does not such a music then immediately also acquire the very same problems and contradictions which the serious avant garde has to face? And indeed, does it not acquire an even bigger problem – that is, the practical problem presented by a 'radical' music which still tries to remain popular (or a 'popular' music which also aims to be radical)? The question is, to what extent and for how long is such a music able to maintain its knife-edge position in the tension between the two opposites (as they have now become)? And is it able to withstand the strong tendency to fall into being either popular or radical, unable to be both at the same time? The difficulty lies not only in the music itself; it lies even more in the demands made upon the music by the culture industry. Ultimately decisive is not whatever aims the music itself might have, but rather the way in which the music is consumed in spite of those aims. For, although the possibility of critical self-reflection within popular music indicates that it might be able, perhaps, to neutralize at least some of the effects of the culture industry (depending as these do on the manipulation and mystification of the relations between the production, reproduction and reception of music), there are few signs to show that this has actually been achieved to any lasting extent. Increasingly sophisticated mechanisms of marketing and distribution make it ever more difficult for any music – whether serious or popular, traditional or avant-garde, Western or non-Western – to resist its fate as commodity. If a radical popular music attempts to renounce consumption and aspires towards the predicament of the serious avant garde, it immediately runs the risk of alienating itself from the general public, and then becomes a minority music which can no longer be regarded as popular (the predicament of much contemporary jazz). It can then be considered 'popular' only in the very limited sense that it makes use of the elements of popular music material. It will not be popular in terms of ratings in the charts.

It is doubtful, moreover, whether the kind of 'unreconciled middle way' represented by Kurt Weill's music in the 1930s can any longer provide an escape from polarization towards either of the two extremes. Even in the early 1930s Adorno had hinted that the songs from *The Threepenny Opera* could well end up being taken quite simply as hit songs in spite of the composer's intentions, and thus could be easily absorbed by the culture industry.[29] It is also significant that, after his emigration to the United States, Weill became, quite unambiguously, a popular music composer. To stretch the Weill analogy somewhat and apply it to Frank Zappa: in the earlier records (*Freak Out!*, *We're Only In It For The Money*, *Absolutely Free*) Zappa and The Mothers of Invention succeeded in performing a remarkable balancing act between the spheres of popular and of radical music – largely through the creative use of parody and Brecht-like alienation techniques as well as elements from twentieth-century serious music. Some of the later records, however, appeared at times to sacrifice this tension, either for a more obviously popular appeal (lengthy virtuoso guitar solos, and moments when parody comes so close to the thing being parodied as to be almost indistinguishable from it), or for the questionable desire to join the serious avant garde itself.[30]

So we have come full-circle. Although Adorno's theory may contain a 'hidden potential' which allows for a radical, critical and self-reflective popular music, such a music must then inevitably come right up against the contradiction most central to Adorno's argument: the alienation faced by all avant-garde music, no matter what the sources of its musical material, in the increasing split

[29] See Adorno, 'Zur gesellschaftlichen Lage der Musik', p.122.
[30] See Ben Watson, *Frank Zappa: The Negative Dialectics of Poodle Play* (London: Quartet Books, 1994) for a different view.

between the two categories (examined at the beginning of this essay) of, on the one hand, music which accepts its fate as commodity and, on the other, music which opposes this. If Adorno's diagnosis of the predicament of music in the twentieth century is correct – which, in its main features, I consider it to be – then a critical, self-reflective music using the material of popular music can no more escape the contradiction formulated by Adorno than can the serious avant garde. This is not to say that the change of function which has taken place within certain areas of popular music and jazz – so that there can be movement from category one to category two as well as in the opposite direction – is not significant. Nevertheless, it is perhaps even more significant that Adorno's central contradiction still remains and is essentially untouched by these developments.

4 Critical Reflections on Adorno

Adorno's writing on music, in spite of its classic status, remains controversial. To the extent that its importance has been acknowledged to any significant degree within the discipline of music and, in particular, within musicology and music theory, this is largely due to Adorno's indisputable historical position as protagonist of musical modernism, rather than for any particular value accorded to the critical theoretical approach itself. Indeed, theoretically speaking, Adorno on the whole tends to be regarded as a polemicist rather than as a systematic thinker, his work on Wagner and even Beethoven frequently being seen in this light, as well as the admittedly polemical *Philosophy of New Music*. Reasons for this extremely patchy reception within musicology in the English-speaking world are not, of course, difficult to find. They come down to three factors already touched on earlier in this book. One of these is certainly the insular character of musicology itself, and its reluctance to take on the problem of music's larger context in any systematic sense. Related to this, there is a general lack of familiarity with the terms of reference and conceptual framework of Critical Theory. And underlying everything else, there is the perverse intricacy of the writing itself and its legendary resistance to translation or summary. Adorno's thinking (as indeed is the case with his more conservative disciple Carl Dahlhaus) is underpinned by a dialectical mode of operation which is quite foreign to Anglo-American musicology, and this has undoubtedly acted as a barrier to its wider acceptance.

The complexity of the style of the writing, the dialectical method which underlies it, and the calculated exaggerations and the extreme nature of the claims it made for itself, had all served to alienate the central figure of Adorno's writings on music: Arnold Schoenberg himself. Schoenberg had always been suspicious of Adorno and clearly disliked him as a person. He was also decidedly sceptical of Adorno's attempts at a philosophy of music, and very much resented what he took to be a personal attack on his music in *Philosophy of New Music*. At this time of his life Schoenberg was suspicious to an extreme of anyone who did not give him total and unquestioning allegiance, and it is therefore perhaps not so surprising that he should have misunderstood Adorno's intention in the book, mistaking a dialectical analysis of his music for an attack on it. In a letter to H.H. Stuckenschmidt on 5th December 1949 he wrote:

> So modern music has a philosophy – it would be enough if it had a philosopher. He attacks me quite vehemently in it. Another disloyal person . . . I have never been able to bear the fellow . . . now I know that he has clearly never liked my music . . . it is disgusting, by the way, how he treats Stravinsky. I am certainly no admirer of Stravinsky, although I like a piece of his here and there very much – but one should not write like that.[1]

And later the same day Schoenberg wrote in a letter to Rufer:

> The book is very difficult to read, for it uses this quasi-philosophical jargon in which modern professors of philosophy hide the absence

[1] H.H. Stuckenschmidt, *Schoenberg: His Life, World and Work*, trans. Humphrey Searle (London: Calder, 1977), p.508.

of an idea. They think it is profound when they produce lack of clarity by undefined new expressions . . . naturally he knows all about twelve-tone music, but he has no idea of the creative process . . . He seems to believe that the twelve-tone row, if it doesn't hinder thought, hinders invention – the poor fellow . . . the book will give many of my enemies a handle, especially because it is so scientifically done.[2]

Schoenberg's criticisms leave us in no doubt that they are coloured by his general mistrust and personal dislike of Adorno. Particularly the remark that 'he has no idea of the creative process' may be considered unwarranted, in view of Adorno's studies with Bernhard Sekles (Hindemith's composition teacher in Frankfurt), Eduard Steuermann[3] and Alban Berg, and the evidence offered by his own compositions.[4] Nevertheless, Schoenberg's diatribes do contain in a nutshell most of the objections which crop up, in one form or another, in the writings of Adorno's critics. Underlying the composer's complaints is probably the most fundamental reservation of all – that concerning what he saw as the questionable nature of a philosophical approach to music in the first place. Contained here is both the practical musician's mistrust of high-flown philosophical theory about music and the musicologist's sceptical attitude to speculation without a firm empirical basis (although there is a certain irony in Schoenberg's objections, given the highly speculative and metaphysical undercarriage to his own *Theory of Harmony* of 1911 – the parts, that is, that were omitted from the first English translation because the

[2] Ibid.

[3] Regarding the high estimation in which Adorno was held by the pianist Eduard Steuermann, see Eduard Steuermann, 'Briefe an Theodor W. Adorno', *Zeugnisse: Theodor W. Adorno zum 60. Geburtstag*, ed. Max Horkheimer (Frankfurt/Main: Europäische Verlagsanstalt, 1963), p.360.

[4] Adorno's compositions are published in two volumes as: T.W. Adorno, *Kompositionen*, ed., Heinz-Klaus Metzger and Rainer Riehn (Munich: Edition Text + Kritik, 1980). A number of his works have also been recorded and are available as *Theodor W. Adorno: Kompositionen*, on CD Wergo WER 6173-2). The influence of Berg is pronounced.

publishers considered them 'too philosophical'). Then there is the harshness of Adorno's criticism of music which does not fall easily into the Austro–German mould (e.g. Stravinsky and, importantly, jazz and popular music). The complexity and obscurity of his prose style, and his use of jargon and foreign words (often seen as élitism and snobbishness) are the most immediately striking features of Adorno's writing, together with its lack of what generally may be regarded as an empirical foundation (and in musical terms, the tendency to go far beyond the bounds of purely technical analysis). Of concern also is the direction in which his theory leads – its 'meaning', if any; and the nature of its utopian vision. And importantly, there is the apparently radical character of his thought which, it has been argued, may only serve to further the interests of the *status quo* (e.g. Schoenberg's complaint that 'the book will give many of my enemies a handle'; but the same contradiction, seen in a political context, also provided the point of departure for Adorno's critics from the New Left). To this list must also be added objections to the value-loaded and transcendent elements of his philosophy; the tendency, in spite of its claims to the contrary, towards systematiz-ation; and his unrelenting seriousness and pessimism. Looking at any one of these criticisms will quickly involve us in a consider-ation of all the others.

1. Values and Prejudices

What strikes one immediately about the tone of Adorno's writing is its absolute seriousness of purpose – its absence of 'illusion and play', of *Schein und Spiel* as he terms it in *Philosophy of New Music*. Everything counts, everything is significant. Adorno's writing itself naturally parallels what he considers to be music's essential seriousness of purpose and necessary tautness of construction, and this, combined with what has often been seen as his élitism, partic-ularly in relation to popular musics, has done much to hinder a more general acceptance of his ideas. As Wesley Blomster has rather tactfully put it: 'it is felt that a greater humility might have vastly increased his effectiveness'.[5] And his extreme seriousness, which can often come across as arrogance, is by no means, of course, peculiar only to Adorno. It is to be encountered as a feature of German theoretical and philosophical writing in general. From another angle it can be viewed as a tendency to take a promising hypothesis to that extreme point where it seems to go considerably beyond the realms of any practical application, and to become so all-embracing and abstract to risk verging on the absurd. Combined with this feature there usually goes, tradition-ally, a prose style of horrifying complexity (although to such tempting generalizations there are notable exceptions – the clarity of Karl Kraus,[6] for example, on whose prose style Schoenberg had so avidly modelled his own). These elements are perhaps to be connected with the particularly German obsession with unity and the organic interrelatedness of parts to whole. In the attempt to describe the intricacies of what is essentially an almost mystical vision of unity in multiplicity which runs through German art and philosophy,[7] and in the desire to account for everything, it is not so surprising that the limits of the empirical and of the everyday, common-sense view of the world should be overstepped and language itself strained beyond its capacity to cope. After the moment of inspiration comes its development, its working-out,

[5] Wesley Blomster, 'Sociology of Music: Adorno and Beyond', *Telos* No. 28 (1976), p.109 Note.

[6] Karl Kraus (1874-1936) opposed through his writings and lectures the barbarism into which he considered the German language was regressing through journalism and increasing use of jargon. Schoenberg was an avid disciple of his prose style, while Berg, accompanied by the young Adorno, never missed his lectures in Vienna in the 1920s.

[7] It is often forgotten that many of the terms used to denote philosophical concepts within the German Idealist tradition have their origin in the attempts of the German mystic Meister Eckhart (1260-1327) to formulate the mystical experience. His legacy to German philosophy has been profound and long lasting.

its materialization in time. Adorno comments that 'German ideology demands that this precise moment of inspiration be concealed: it is the domination of the artist over nature which is to appear as nature itself.'[8] He writes perceptively of this ideological aspect of German music, where original inspiration is not something made, or developed in itself; it is something 'given', an experience of wholeness which cannot be reduced further. With the subsequent development of this given experience, so he suggests in *Philosophy of New Music*, goes the need to hide its exact point of occurrence and at the same time to make everything else within the work seem permeated by that original inspiration. By skill and craftsmanship every other moment in the work is made to appear at the same level as the inspired moment. The danger is that of systematization, and in the attempt to clarify totally (in terms of total development of the possibilities inherent in the inspired moment) there is the risk both of obscuring the original vision and of extending it too far. But in attempting to free thought and experience from total systematization and reification, Adorno's own work can also be seen as itself coming close to systematization. The tendency to over-extension and the obsession with 'unity through multiplicity' are particular features of German Idealist philosophy, with its assumption of transcendent values (and Marxism results, in part, from a critique of, and dialogue with, this tradition.) These values, whether in terms of *Geist* or of Utopia, would seem to contain, almost in spite of themselves, an invitation for ideological exploitation. That Adorno was aware of this should go without saying: one of the central concerns of his work is the attempt to unmask this tendency of philosophy, art and science unwittingly to be assimilated by dominant ideologies.[9]

---

[8] Adorno, *Philosophy of Modern Music*, trans. Anne G. Mitchell and Wesley Blomster (New York: Seabury Pres, 1973), p.185.

[9] Adorno himself had been compromised in this respect when, in 1934, he published a review in *Die Musik* which appeared to comment favourably on the score of a work for male-voice choir by Herbert Müntzel, settings of poems by

Nevertheless, in spite of his own efforts to avoid the dangers that go with grand philosophical designs, and in spite of the antisystematic nature of Critical Theory, it is disturbing that elements of authoritarianism are to be discerned in Adorno's own work. It is to this aspect that his more savage critics have pointed with obvious satisfaction. John Shepherd, for example, in his early essay 'The Meaning of Music', describes Adorno as 'a man, who despite his radical pose, betrays the authoritarianism implicit in many élitist European academic systems'.[10] And even Wesley Blomster, who is generally sympathetic to Adorno's work, admits that 'there are moments of uneasiness in working with Adorno when one finds in his position the imprint of that "authoritarian personality" which he himself fought so vehemently'.[11] The extreme tone of his writing has a tendency to take on the colour of what it attacks, and Adorno himself sometimes demonstrates the kinds of irrational prejudice he so acutely points to in others. All this indicates yet again to the need for Adorno to be examined in the light of his own theory, otherwise much that is of great value in his work will be discarded along with its more unacceptable features.

Adorno's work on jazz and popular music is undoubtedly marred by the fact that he himself detested such music. Because of this, even the valid elements of his criticism in this area can easily be interpreted as mere justification of his own prejudices. A striking example of this is the suggestion that Adorno enthusiastically

---

[9] (cont.)
the Nazi poet Baldur von Schirach. But to argue that this indicated support for the Nazis is patently absurd, given the testimony of his life's work against authoritarianism. See Adorno, *Gesammelte Schriften* 19 (Frankfurt am Main: Suhrkamp, 1984), pp.331-2; also pp.637-8.

[10] John Shepherd, 'The Meaning of Music', in *Whose Music? A Sociology of Musical Languages* (London: Latimer, 1977), p.65.

[11] Wesley Blomster, 'Sociology of Music: Adorno and Beyond', p.109. Blomster is referring here to the psychological study Adorno coordinated and co-authored in the United States, *The Authoritarian Personality* (1950).

supported the Nazi ban on jazz in the early days of the Third Reich.[12] This certainly constitutes an opportunistic misreading of what is admittedly a rather strident early article, 'Abschied vom Jazz'[13] of 1933. While Adorno was probably foolish, with hindsight, to have taken the Nazis' 1933 ban on the broadcasting of jazz (which they labelled 'Negerjazz') as a starting point for his article, his argument certainly cannot be construed as supporting the Nazis. Indeed, two of the key points he makes are that jazz (by which, as we have established in Chapter Three, he means commercial dance band music and hit songs), beneath its veneer, has a rhythmic scheme uncomfortably close to that of the military march (an ironic and thinly disguised reference to the Nazis' own love of martial music), and that jazz in this sense has little to do with black music, being rather a commercial exploitation of 'negro music' by whites. As we have seen, because his listening experience of jazz and popular music, like most Europeans at that time, appeared to have been limited almost exclusively to what he heard on the radio, Adorno was unable to see the music as anything other than debased and degenerated forms of traditional (serious) music.[14] He seemed to be so identified with his own cultural heritage and its aesthetic values that he was quite blind to the different terms of reference of any non-European let alone non-Western culture. That jazz and popular music could be regarded as having, at least in part, different roots and values did not seriously seem to have occurred to him, or that it could have a critical or subversive element. This has led to a particularly strong rejection of this area of Adorno's work by theorists who otherwise embrace the Critical Theory of the Frankfurt School. As Bernard Gendron has commented in his article 'Theodor Adorno meets the Cadillacs':

[12] See Michael H. Kater, *Different Drummers: Jazz in the Culture of Nazi Germany* (New York & Oxford: Oxford University Press, 1992), p.33.

[13] T.W. Adorno, 'Abschied vom Jazz' (1933), in *Gesammelte Schriften* 18 (Frankfurt am Main! Suhrkamp, 1984), pp.795-799.

[14] See also Gillian Rose, *The Melanchohly Science*, p.134.

113

Many of the present generation of culture theorists took part in the radical movements of the sixties, which turned to rock'n'roll as their primary means of cultural expression and turned to the Frankfurt School for their first lessons in culture theory. Not surprisingly, these new theorists display an ambivalence towards popular culture that is virtually nonexistent in the work of Adorno, Marcuse, and the rest. Although they agree that the products of the culture industry play a crucial role in buttressing the domination of patriarchal capitalism, they insist that in the right circumstances these products can also be put to a subversive use. For many, rock'n'roll's appearance at a particular juncture of class, generational, and cultural struggle has given it a preeminent role among mass cultural artifacts as an instrument of opposition and liberation,[15]

But at the same time, of course, Adorno's theory of mass culture is required reading for any serious study of popular music, and the approach he put forward is path-breaking and cannot be ignored. Its weaknesses lie in its overgeneralizations, its lack of detailed differentiation, and in the fact that it is firmly rooted in a particular historical period – the inter-war years, when Tin Pan Alley ruled supreme. Richard Middleton, in a thorough-going critique of Adorno's position on popular music which also emphasizes its fundamental importance to to the larger development of theories of mass culture,[16] considers that the Critical Theory of the Frankfurt School tended to overstate the homogeneity of the ruling structure, in terms of a unity of state, administrative and economic apparatuses while at the same time underplaying the influence of class-related tensions. In this he is certainly correct, in that, in the case of Adorno and Horkheimer in particular, this was the result of

[15] Bernard Gendron, 'Theodor Adorno meets the Cadillacs', in T. Modelski (ed.), *Studies in Entertainment: Critical Approaches to Mass Culture* (Bloomington: Indiana, 1986), p.10.

[16] Richard Middleton, ' "It's all over now. Popular music and mass culture – Adorno's theory', *Studying Popular Music* (Milton Keynes: Open University Press. 1990), pp.34-63.

a generalized and rather extreme application of Max Weber's concept of rationalization which led to the formulation of a notion of the 'culture industry' which was all powerful, centralized and all controlling, and which assumed, as Simon Frith has pointed out, total passivity at the level of reception/consumption.[17] Middleton, drawing on Frith, argues that 'what is missed is that alongside an increase in centralized control has been persistent dissent; domination – social, economic and ideological – has been maintained only through *struggle*'.[18] As examples of this he points to the rise of independent record companies and the constant conflicts between musicians and the major multi-national record companies. Like Frith, he argues that there is a constant pressure from the grass roots to which the record companies have no choice but respond, and which cannot simply be explained by Adorno's concept of 'pseudo-individualization'. Adorno's theory cannot account for changes in taste, and Middleton suggests that all that record companies can do is to try to cover as many areas of taste as possible, even if this inevitably leads to overproduction on a massive scale. As he says: 'Companies certainly try to control demand, to channel it in known directions, but they are never *sure* of their market'.[19] To this extent there is certainly an element of subversiveness and unpredictability in the consumption of popular music which can also be seen to influence its production and distribution in ways that remained unrecognized by Adorno as the result of a certain cultural blindness.

Aspects of the analysis of Stravinsky's music in Adorno's theory of aesthetic modernism may also be seen as the product of a similar tunnel vision. Stravinsky's music – apart from being at the opposite extreme to that of Schoenberg, both considered as different tendencies within the European tradition – may also be regarded as having its roots in quite different musical soil. It is

[17] See Simon Frith, *Sound Effects: Youth, leisure, and the politics of rock'n'roll* (London: Constable, 1983), p.45.

[18] Richard Middleton, *Studying Popular Music*, p.37 (italics in original).

[19] Ibid., p.38 (italics in original).

possible to argue that those elements of which Adorno is so highly critical in Stravinsky's music, and which he regards as regressive – for example, its impersonal character and lack of expression, its static quality, the incessant repetition of melodic fragments with constantly changing rhythmic emphasis, the delight in ritual, the use of masks and the changing of roles (as, for example, in *Renard*) – are precisely those features which distinguish the music of many non-European cultures from the tradition of European Classical and Romantic music. Furthermore, much non-Western music actually achieves its 'expressive' effect precisely through a lack of overt expression (for example, Balinese music, or the Buddhist temple music of Tibet), and this hieratic element is to be recognized also in the music of Stravinsky. In fact Adorno seems to touch on this when he writes: 'The empty eyes of his [Stravinsky's] music have at times more expression than does expression itself'.[20] Russia, from its isolated position on the edges of Europe and Asia, came late to European art music, and in so doing contributed much that was new and exotic (although it was the French who were most immediately responsive to these influences, whereas Austria-Germany remained largely unaffected). Stravinsky, as a Russian, seemed able from the beginning to approach the legacy of the European musical tradition with a certain detachment, a lack of identification which Schoenberg, immersed in the heart of that culture, could never show. Stravinsky is able to manipulate his material in the detached and 'objective' way he does precisely because of his lack of identification with it. What were for Schoenberg almost sacred elements of European art music – the need for organic unity achieved from within the material itself, for example – could not, considering his different heritage, have the same significance for Stravinsky. In what Adorno criticizes as a lack of a sense of the historical dimension of the material, and also as a lack of creativity, can be seen

[20] Adorno, *Philosophy of Modern Music*, p.177.

116

from another perspective in fact as exactly what distinguishes Stravinsky in this century. That is to say, it is only in the twentieth-century that it has become possible to take the kind of 'objective' and eclectic (though in Adorno's terms, irresponsible and dilettantish) view of history represented by Stravinsky's neo-classicism – a factor which Stravinsky's music shares with postmodernism. In this connection Hans Vogt has argued that:

> [Stravinsky] has been accused, on many counts, of not being genuinely creative and of being capable basically only of writing 'music about music'... Such criticism overlooks, in my opinion, the... 'presence of tradition' (*Traditionspräsenz*), which only became possible in the intellectual climate of the twentieth century, and which one could call post-historicist. For this to be effectively put into productive work is, at least as far as music is concerned, a new intellectual conception, without precedent and therefore creative. It is remarkable that even Adorno was totally blind regarding this characteristic.[21]

Underlying this dispute is a very particular notion of musical material – a concept which is so fundamental to Adorno's critical theory of music that it calls for a more detailed consideration here.

2. The Concept of Musical Material: Some Issues

Although it is perhaps questionable to talk of 'central concepts' in a philosophy which determinedly rejects philosophical 'first things', there is nevertheless a strong case for arguing that the one concept in Adorno's critical aesthetics of music to which all others gravitate is the concept of 'musical material'. I would argue that much of the controversy which Adorno's music theory has attracted – and continues to attract – can be traced back precisely

[21] Hans Vogt, *Neue Musik seit 1945* (Stuttgart: Reclam, 1972), p.239. See also Alfred Huber, 'Adornos Polemik gegen Stravinsky', *Melos* 9 (1971), p.356ff.

to this single concept, particularly as it is formulated in *Philosophy of New Music*. When the book appeared in 1949 – a significant year for the development of the European avant garde, marked by Messiaen's *Modes de valeurs et d'intensités*, the precursor of total serialism – Adorno's concept of musical material came immediately to have a considerable influence on the post-war Darmstadt composers. But the significance of the notion of a 'dialectic of musical material' pre-dates *Philosophy of New Music* (it can be traced back to Adorno's early writings from the 1920s[22]), and concerns not only twentieth-century music from the perspective of an avant garde. This perspective fundamentally shapes Adorno's view of music of the whole 'bourgeois period', from the early eighteenth century up to the mid-twentieth century, and also, importantly, it shapes his critique of popular music. The centre of gravity of the concept certainly lies in the nineteenth century, however, in particular with the music of Beethoven and Wagner.[23]

The concept of musical material is central to Adorno's music theory because it is within the material that he sees the mediation of music and society as taking place in musical terms. That is to say, the mediation of the individual, autonomous work by the heteronomy of the social totality is understood by Adorno in Hegelian terms as the 'objectification of the Subject'. As he puts it in his article 'Klassik, Romantik, neue Musik', 'art always implies the dialectical relationship of a Subject to that which faces it, its material. The objectivity [of art] arises in the first instance from the multiple mediations of this relationship.'[24] In essence, therefore, Adorno's theory of musical material, as mediated 'second nature', is also a theory of form. I have argued elsewhere

[22] See Max Paddison, *Adorno's Aesthetics of Music*, Chapter 2 for an account of the development of the concept and its prehistory.

[23] Ibid., pp.218-62.

[24] Adorno, *Klangfiguren* (1959) in *Gesammelte Schriften* 16 (Frankfurt/Main: Suhrkamp, 1978), p.128 (my trans.).

that the concept of form needs to be understood on two levels: the 'pre-formation' of the material, as handed-down genres, forms and schemata; and the 'formation' – i.e., re-contextualization – of this pre-formed material within the structure of the autonomous work.[25]

Furthermore, Adorno's theory of musical material is also, in effect, a theory of the avant garde, in Adorno's sense of the term rather than that of Peter Bürger, in that the material of music is always taken as that of the present, at the furthest point of development of expressive needs and technical means, while music of the past is to be understood from the position of the most advanced contemporary music. At the same time it also needs to be seen as a theory of mass culture, in that it simultaneously emphasizes the effect of patterns of consumption on musical production, in terms of what he calls the historical disintegration of musical material. In this sense, therefore, the concept of material, like that of mediation which underlies it, is dynamic and historical rather than static and 'natural' in character. Nevertheless, it has also been argued that there is an element of stasis to be detected in the concept of material – as, indeed, in Adorno's philosophy of history itself – to the extent that the historical tendency of the material is not straightforwardly continuous, 'progressive' and integrative, but is also characterized by discontinuities, by regression, and by disintegration.

One commentator to argue this has been Rose Rosengard Subotnik,[26] who asserts that 'Adorno's principal composite image of nineteenth-century music is not that of a historical process but rather one of a static structure'.[27] But this is a questionable

---

[25] Max Paddison, *Adorno's Aesthetics of Music*, pp.149–58.

[26] See Rose Rosengard Subotnik, 'The Historical Structure: Adorno's "French" Model for the Criticism of Nineteenth-Century Music', in *Developing Variations: Style and Ideology in Western Music* (Minneapolis & Oxford: University of Minnesota Press, 1991).

[27] Ibid., p.207.

assertion, substituting as it does a static structuralist model for Adorno's dynamic dialectical one, on the grounds of his emphasis on discontinuity and on the shift from temporal processes towards spacial structures in the course of the nineteenth century. This runs the risk of hypostasizing discontinuity at the expense of a continuity which still maintains an important and necessary presence in Adorno's dialectical analysis. I would suggest that it is not so much a question of static structures as of sudden and discontinuous change, and that any sense of ongoing historical movement needs to be understood more in terms of a spiral process than a straight line of development. Nevertheless, Subotnik's structuralist reading of Adorno does provide valuable insights, in terms of the relation between, on the one hand, the increasing fragmentation of nineteenth-century music and its culmination in the disintegration of twentieth-century Modernism, and, on the other, the perceived wholeness of eighteenth-century Classicism. Subotnik writes:

> Thus the terminus that Adorno most frequently indicates for nineteenth-century music is Schoenberg's twelve-tone music, the culmination of a historical process whereby Schoenberg, to follow Adorno's account, derives from Brahms precisely the unifying principle Wagner needed – though only to show that the one basis of integrity left in the modern world is lack of wholeness.[28]

It is the concept of rationalization, more than any other idea, which underpins Adorno's and Horkheimer's critical analysis of Western culture in *Dialectic of Enlightenment*, which informs Adorno's concept of the historical dialectic of musical material, and which is to be seen in particularly extreme form in *Philosophy of New Music*, in terms of the concepts of progress and regression and the Schoenberg-Stravinsky polarization. Richard J. Bernstein has suggested that Adorno and Horkheimer may have

[28] Ibid., p.208.

120

misinterpreted Max Weber's concept of rationalization in some respects, and have seen in it the notion of historical inevitability.[29] This view could certainly find support in the connection Adorno clearly made between the process of rationalization and Schoenberg's idea of historical necessity in the relation to musical material.

Of a different type – although also pointing to its ideological character – is the kind of criticism of Adorno's concept of material which argues that it represents a kind of 'Custer's last stand' of the bourgeoisie.[30] Konrad Boehmer is probably the most emphatic representative of this view. Boehmer criticizes Adorno's concept of material for simply reflecting the historical demise of bourgeois art music as the negation of musical production. He writes:

> His concept of material is nevertheless thoroughly reactionary because it has not analysed the bourgeois conditions underlying this specific form of musical praxis but has simply glorified them. His negation is the affirmation of the aporias of the late bourgeois period.[31]

There are also difficulties with Adorno's use of Hegel's concept of 'Objective Spirit' [*objektiver Geist*] to suggest that the relationship between composer and material is not simply a personal and individual relationship, to do only with the expression of the individual Subject, but rather that the interaction is also a collective, supra-individual process. The 'historical dialectic of musical material' rather than the production of individual works therefore becomes the indicator of progress in music. One result of this is that the musical material appears to acquire a kind of self-locomotion. Its historical movement happens apparently without any human

[29] See Richard J. Bernstein (ed.), *Habermas and Modernity* (Cambridge: Polity Press, 1985), p.6.

[30] See Chapter 2, Note 67.

[31] Konrad Boehmer, 'Der Korrepetitor am Werk – Probleme des Material-begriffs bei Adorno', *Zeitschrift für Musiktheorie* 4 (1973), p.32.

agency; or, seen the other way round, individual musical works are regarded as executors of the progress of the musical material/ 'Objective Spirit', in the process becoming thoroughly anthropomorphized.

Implied in Adorno's concept of material there is a methodology, the terms of which I have identified earlier in this book under the categories of technical analysis, sociological critique and philosophical-historical interpretation.[32] I have argued that this implied model is of real value for the understanding of music in its material relationship to complex modern societies. At the same time, however, I have also suggested elsewhere[33] that there are problems in the use of such a model. The difficulties lie in the fuzziness of the categories, so that they either leak into one another, making clear distinctions difficult to establish, or they leave one sometimes with the feeling that the connections between them have been made by a sleight of hand. This problem did not escape Dahlhaus's notice. He observed that:

> The concept of musical material is a compositional/technical and simultaneously an aesthetic, historical/philosophical and sociological category.... The different moments which are included within the concept of material flow into one another. In Adorno's aesthetic theory, which sets itself in opposition to the scientific division of disciplines, compositional/technical arguments are turned, without further ado, into historical/ philosophical or sociological ones, without clear boundaries being drawn.[34]

And overall, the concept of musical material is firmly tied to a particular tradition of Western art music. The fact that Adorno was so immersed in the tradition of Austro-Germany, and the fact

[32] See Chapter 2.

[33] See Max Paddison, *Adorno's Aesthetics of Music*, p.277.

[34] Carl Dahlhaus, 'Adornos Begriff des musikalischen Materials', in *Zur Terminologie der Musik des 20. Jahrhunderts Bericht über das zweite Kolloquium*, ed. H.H. Eggebrecht (Stuttgart, 1974), p.13.

that he showed so little interest in the different values of other, non-European cultures, means that he laid himself open to the criticism of imposing essentially subjective and relative values as if they were objective and universal. Trevor Wishart, in his essay 'On Radical Culture',[35] maintains that Adorno is caught in the trap of having to defend his own 'intellectual property', and can thereby be accused of fetishizing culture. Adorno can therefore be seen as guilty of what he himself criticizes in Valéry[36] – that is, that the assumption of cultural values is a form of marketing technique. Wishart also considers that Adorno adopts an evaluative position (particularly to be seen in his use of terms like 'authentic' and 'true') which gives the appearance of transcending the social situation. In doing this Adorno is apparently placing himself outside the society he is criticizing, and is therefore indulging in an abstraction, divorced from life as lived. In spite of all his claims to be examining the art work in its relation to society, he in fact ends up, according to Wishart, by elevating art and aesthetics to a position apart from their essentially class-based, economic context. Adorno can thus be accused of having vested interests, and of being determined, through his criticism of bourgeois culture, to perpetuate the *status quo* rather than attempting to change it. From Wishart's viewpoint, Adorno's pose is pseudo-radical: in not acknowledging its own class-role and in appealing to a spurious objectivity it is in reality intent on preserving the position of an isolated, intellectual élite. It cannot be denied that this is the kind of impression that Adorno's work often creates. At the same time it must be remembered that negative dialectics does not pretend to be a form of relativism. If its underlying conceptual framework and its associated values are rejected, then Critical Theory itself will split into a multiplicity of contradictory viewpoints which, in the absence of the (albeit unstated)

[35] Trevor Wishart, 'On Radical Culture', in *Whose Music?*, p.234.

[36] Ibid., p.234. Cf Adorno, 'Cultural Criticism and Society', in *Prisms*, trans. Samuel and Shierry Weber (London: Neville Spearman, 1967), pp.22-3.

centre implied and pointed to by these values, will indeed become meaningless. Wishart criticizes Adorno for implying that the public has an obligation to try to understand the artist; that is, 'that art accords with some socially-external laws of meaningfulness, truth etc., while it is our responsibility to judge it against these laws . . . rather than that the artist or critic has an obligation to convey his meaning to the public, i.e. that a work is only meaningful via its social existence'.[37] This is the kind of straight-forward either/or ultimatum that Adorno's stand constantly invites, and which at the same time it resists. For Adorno, the work of art is both a social fact and at the same time something which has a critical function in relation to social reality by virtue of its historically acquired autonomy from immediate social function. It is from the creative tension between these two poles, so he insists, that the significance of art springs. Much of the kind of criticism which Adorno attracts would appear to be an attempt to avoid this tension through polarization to either one of its extremes. This is a particular feature of those who criticize Adorno on ideological or political grounds.

3. Politics and Protest

The most bitter criticisms against Adorno have always been to do with the perceived ideological and political content of his work. Adorno's lectures in Frankfurt in the 1960s (and also those of his one-time colleague Herbert Marcuse at the same period in the United States) became the rallying-point of the New Left student movement. The students saw in Adorno's analyses of society, and particularly in his sociological interpretations of art, not only a revelation of the hidden workings of society but also the promise of something better – the realization of the potential contained within society's decline. It seemed to them that if such a potential

[37] Trevor Wishart, 'On Radical Culture', p.238.

existed already – as, for example, to be seen in the 'promise of happiness' contained in art – then so also must it be possible to realize this potential, in reality and immediately, within society itself. While Marcuse (whose musical tastes, unlike Adorno's, tended towards the affirmative culture of nineteenth-century Italian opera) viewed similar developments in America as something to be encouraged, Adorno and Horkheimer were disturbed by the turn events were taking in Frankfurt. They had never considered Critical Theory to be a model for political action, and were repelled by the possibility of their ideas being an excuse for the use of violence to bring about political change. Adorno's statement at that time – 'I had set up a theoretical model, but I could not suspect that people would want to put it into action with Molotov cocktails'[38] – has often been cited. Adorno saw the aim of Critical Theory as bringing about a change in consciousness (and thus also, by implication, in social reality) rather than directly attempting to change society itself, and he maintained that this was the level on which his theory must remain. When students demanded to know what should be done, in terms of political praxis, Adorno's answer was simply that he did not know. His students became disillusioned. His lectures on dialectics were disrupted in 1968, and he was denounced by revolutionary students distributing a leaflet entitled 'Adorno as an institution is dead'.[39] In an interview with Der Spiegel shortly after these events Adorno is quoted as saying:

Philosophy in so far as it remains philosophy cannot recommend direct steps or changes. It brings about changes in so far as it remains theory. I think that for once the question might well be asked whether it is not a form of opposition for a man to think and write the things that I write. Is not theory also a genuine form of practice?[40]

[38] Adorno, 'Of Barricades and Ivory Towers – An Interview with T.W. Adorno', *Encounter* 33 (September 1969), p.63.
[39] Ibid., p.65.
[40] Ibid., p.68

Konrad Boehmer (one of the most vociferous of Adorno's critics to emerge from the New Left of the 1960s) insists that, no matter what its object is, Adorno's sociology of music 'is measured against the music of the bourgeois epoch, a music whose eminent political function was to withdraw once and for all from any type of political subordination into a position of autonomy where it might fully develop and differentiate.'[41] He maintains that Adorno failed to come to terms with social reality in his own age and with the social foundation of its art by dwelling so narrowly on the musical aspects of the bourgeoisie. Boehmer further maintains that Adorno had not rigorously analysed the relation between music and society, and he criticizes Adorno's analysis of the conditions of the production of music. He considers that, although Adorno accomplished much, he never asked the most fundamental question – i.e., what produced those conditions. This question, according to Boehmer, would shed light on the class character of music, no matter how much the musical products themselves might deny it.[42] Similar criticisms have been levelled at Adorno's attempt to categorize various response styles to the experience of music (for example in *Philosophy of New Music* [43] and in the opening chapter of *Introduction to the Sociology of Music* [44]). The criticism is that Adorno did not really go very far in his examination of response styles, and that in fact his typology is not the result of empirical research into the real situation as it exists, but demonstrates instead the same kind of prejudices and reification that it attempts to criticize.[45] Wishart complains that Adorno does not make any real attempt to get to the root of the matter, which would be to try

[41] Konrad Boehmer, *Texte zur Musiksoziologie*, p.227; cited in Blomster, 'Sociology of Music: Adorno and Beyond', p.110.

[42] Ibid., p.232; cited in Blomster, p.110.

[43] Adorno, *Philosophy of Modern Music*, pp.197–201.

[44] Adorno, *Introduction to the Sociology of Music*, pp.1–20. Adorno's typology includes: the 'expert', the 'good listener', the 'culture consumer', the 'emotional listener', the 'sensuous listener', and the 'resentment listener'.

[45] Cf. Gillian Rose, *The Melancholy Science*, p.134.

to discover the social bases of authentic response styles. The reason is, in his opinion, that 'this would involve venturing beyond the secure sphere of intellectual speculation towards an investigation of reality, towards praxis...and hence the necessity of deserting the secure world of bourgeois academic cultural criticism against which he rails'.[46]

Adorno's reply to this kind of criticism in general was that empirically it is not possible to measure the *quality* of the response to the experience of music, but merely the *intensity*, which in reality tells one very little of any value. Nevertheless, he does invite empirical research into the questions he raises speculatively in *Introduction to the Sociology of Music*, including the famous typology of listeners in its opening chapter. The book, it needs to be remembered, was originally a series of lectures on the sociology of music delivered at Frankfurt University, and in the Preface to the book he writes:

> The lectures themselves occasionally touch on the relation to empirical sociology. The author is conceited enough to believe that he is supplying the musical branch of that discipline with enough fruitful questions to keep it meaningfully occupied for some time and to advance the link between theory and fact-finding – a link that is constantly called for and constantly put off again, not without changes in the overly abstract polarity of both occurring in the process. But he is not conceited enough to posit, as already valid, whatever theses of his might be plausible in theory, insofar as they imply empirical assertions. By empirical rules, many of those would be hypothetical. At times – in the typology, for instance – it is fairly clear how research techniques might serve to test the ideas; in other chapters, as in the ones on function or on public opinion, it is less obvious. Working out the process in detail would have exceeded the limits which the author placed on his task.[47]

[46] Trevor Wishart, *Whose Music?*, p.239
[47] Adorno, *Introduction to the Sociology of Music*, p.xi.

However, it has to be said that Adorno seldom worked out such ideas in detail, and as far as testing hypotheses empirically was concerned he was by the 1950s and 1960s quite hostile to the whole tradition of empiricism. Even in the United States in the late 1930s and the 1940s, when he had some engagement with American empirical methodology in sociology and psychology, his attitude to standards of scientific objectivity provoked heart-felt complaints from project collaborators. Paul Lazarsfeld, the sociologist with whom he worked on the Princeton Radio Research Project, wrote to Adorno in late 1939 complaining: 'Your disrespect for possibilities alternative to your own ideas becomes even more disquieting when your text leads to the suspicion that you don't even know how an empirical check upon a hypothetical assumption is made'.[48]

Boehmer's conclusions, like those of Wishart, are that Adorno's sociology of music, even though criticizing bourgeois music, remained dependent upon it, since it never drew the consequences of its criticism. This leads to the view – and it is the view of a number of his critics whether politically committed or not – that Adorno's theory thus becomes a hermetically closed system, which simply goes round in circles without ever coming to the point of committing itself, either in terms of definitive meanings or (in Boehmer's terms) of 'a politically relevant relation of theory and praxis'.[49] The negative aspects of Adorno's critique are thus seen as a dismal admission of impotence and helplessness, a pessimism so complete that any possibility of a solution is smothered in advance. It was taken for granted by Adorno's more politically committed critics in the late 1960s that there were two clear alternatives: either one wishes to perpetuate bourgeois culture and its values; or, one wishes to help it on the way to its inevitable collapse

[48] Letter from Lazarsfeld to Adorno, cited in Martin Jay, *The Dialectical Imagination* (London: Heinemann, 1973), p.223

[49] Konrad Boehmer, *Texte zur Musiksoziologie*, p.237; cited in Blomster, 'Sociology of Music', p.111.

128

in order to establish in its place that ideal, utopian society which present society prevents. To the radical Left, Adorno appeared to be sitting on the fence and therefore, by implication, was serving the purposes of the *status quo* in spite of all he said to the contrary. This is again, of course, the kind of either/or ultimatum that Adorno rejected. He observes in *Minima Moralia* that 'suspicion falls on anyone who combines criticism of capitalism with that of the proletariat'.[50] Nevertheless, the accusation that his theory is, in the final analysis, a hermetic, closed system which leads nowhere, except to a culinary enjoyment of its own intricacies, must be taken seriously. This involves a further consideration of his methodology.

4. System or Anti-System?

It has been frequently emphasized that Adorno's Critical Theory is essentially antisystematic and goes to considerable lengths to avoid grounding itself in any particular system of thought or any set of philosophical givens. In his book *Negative Dialectics* Adorno warns against making the dialectic itself into a philosophical first principle. Susan Buck-Morss, however, considers that Adorno was driven towards this in spite of himself[51] – very much in the way that Schoenberg seemed to be driven inevitably, by the implications of atonality, towards the systematization that resulted in the twelve-tone method. Just as Schoenberg was criticized by Adorno for having once more imprisoned music in the act of freeing it, so can Adorno himself be seen as having once more sealed the fate of philosophy – that is, having led it into a dead end. Susan Buck-Morss also observes that: 'The staticness, the quality of incantation that he so criticized in Benjamin's work was not

---

[50] Adorno, *Minima Moralia*, trans. E.F.N. Jephcott (London NLB, 1974), p.113.

[51] Susan Buck-Morss, *The Origin of Negative Dialectics*, p.190.

lacking in his own'.[52] And she further asks: 'Did the perpetual motion of Adorno's arguments go anywhere? Did they lead out of the bourgeois interieur or simply hang suspended within it like the new art of mobiles?'[53] Taken to its extreme, therefore, antisystematization is in danger itself of becoming a system, even though one of contrasts and of paradox. The internal dynamic of its dialectical argument runs the risk of not leading beyond itself, and thus of degenerating into style. The danger of Adorno's writing becoming an art-form in its own right, a form of literature (or even poetry, as its admirers have been known to consider it) has already been touched on earlier, and it must be admitted that in some respects his prose may become completely satisfying within itself, as within a magic circle. But one cannot help suspecting that Adorno would not have been displeased with such a judgment. Often seen as a composer manqué, he was not merely content in his writing to theorize but, through the use of concrete and vivid images tightly interwoven, he sought to provide an experience which comes close to that of art. Adorno has succeeded in building alienation into the very structure of his texts, in spite of the adulation they excite, in certain quarters, as works of art.

Göran Therborn has suggested that Adorno's view of the world was frozen by the rise of Fascism. Adorno's work, he maintains, in its uncompromising negation, in its refusal to define itself in positive terms, and in its denial of instrumental reason, must be seen in the context of its time as a reaction against authoritarianism. 'Frozen by the Gorgon's head of Fascism,' his negative dialectics was never afterwards able to see the possibility of going beyond its original historical position.[54] Ben

[52] Ibid., p.190.
[53] Ibid., p.190
[54] Göran Therborn, 'The Frankfurt School', *New Left Review* No. 63 (1970), p.94.

Agger[55] take the same view, and considers that Adorno's identification with the music of Schoenberg corroborates this. He writes, in a passage which demonstrates questionable historical accuracy: 'Atonal music evokes the screams of tortured Jews, appropriate to its time.'[56] The general implication seems to be that, in keeping with the mood of alternative optimism displayed in the 1960s and early 1970s, a more affirmative culture is now called for. Agger, like many other critics of the time, was disturbed by Adorno's consistent silence as to the nature of the utopian culture of the future, and as to the kind of music which may point to such a culture. Agger maintains that it is high time that Adorno himself – as prophet of doom – were transcended and his theories re-examined in the light of the changed circumstances of the present. It is quite certain, however, that Adorno would have continued to deny – as he did right to the end of his life – that the situation had changed sufficiently to justify a more optimistic view.

During the period between his death in 1969 and the late 1980s it thus became received wisdom to dismiss Adorno's unremitting cultural pessimism as simply a product of its time – the Weimar Republic, the rise of Hitler, and the Second World War. Göran Therborn's view of Frankfurt School Critical Theory as philosophy caught in the headlights of Fascism typified an influential body of opinion. The judgment – ironic with hindsight – was that, while there was doubtless much to be admired in Adorno's negative dialectics, as a theoretical approach it was quite unable to transcend the horrors of the first half of the twentieth century and demonstrate its relevance to the relative political stability and even optimism of the post sixties cold war years. What is now most striking is how the revolutions which took place across eastern Europe in 1989 and, after a brief moment of confidence, the

[55] Ben Agger, 'On Happiness and the Damaged Life', in *On Critical Theory*, ed. John O'Neill (New York & London: Seabury Press/Heinemann, 1976 1977), pp.12-33.
[56] Ibid., p.32.

instability and upheaval which followed, have led to a climate of thought which in some respects calls to mind the historical period within which Frankfurt School Critical Theory itself originally developed. As in the Europe of the inter-war years, the state of the world at the twentieth century's *fin de siècle* is once again characterized by uncertainty, pessimism and disillusion of a kind which appears to feel some affinity with the Critical Theory of the Frankfurt School and, in particular, with Adorno's version of it. And yet, the music of the post-1989 period has so far shown little readiness or capacity to engage with these uncertainties. On the contrary, the tendency has been to side step the whole issue of a 'crisis', and instead to embrace with evident relief the relativism and stylistic pluralism which have become the hallmark of the new *status quo*. The contradictions raised by this situation provide rich material for a critical theory of music.[57]

The need for critical interpretation and judgment which arises from a dialectical consideration of music both in technical/structural and in contextual/sociological terms seems to me to be a fundamental requirement for any adequate critical method, problematical as it may be to realize such a programme convincingly in concrete terms. In its determination to see the social and the political in music not merely as an adjunct, a function of its context or as a straightforward matter of compositional intent, but instead as something embedded in the very structure of music and its handed-down material, Adorno's Critical Theory continues to make us uncomfortable with received notions of music as splendidly autonomous and somehow entirely separate from society and the everyday. While serious critical scrutiny of his work reveals contradictions and undeniable blind spots, the acuity of his insights and the tenacity of his theoretical approach emerge all the

[57] David Clarke's critical analysis of the music of Arvo Pärt provides a good example of ideology critique in action. See David Clarke, 'Parting Glances: Aesthetic Solace or Act of Complicity,' *Musical Times* (December 1993), pp. 680–84.

more strongly as the result of such a scrutiny. The power of Adorno's critical analysis of music derives in large part from its uncompromisingly modernist form: the way in which it holds its fragmented elements in a kind of dynamic suspension or force-field and refuses to integrate the bits. It is this which prevents the easy appropriation of his approach by a fashionable relativism, and which simultaneously provides the tools for a devastating critique of postmodernist complacency.

Bibliography

For a more complete list of Adorno's writings, particularly those on music, see the Bibliography of my book Adorno's *Aesthetics of Music* (Cambridge: Cambridge University Press, 1993).

1. Works by T.W. Adorno Cited

'The Actuality of Philosophy' (1931), trans. uncredited, *Telos* 31 (1977), pp.120-33

Dialectic of Enlightenment (1947) (with Max Horkheimer). trans. John Cumming (London: Verso, 1979)

'Zur gesellschaftlichen Lage der Musik', *Zeitschrift für Sozialforschung* 1 (1932), pp.103-24 and pp.356-78

'Abschied vom Jazz' (1933), in *Gesammelte Schriften* 18 (Frankfurt am Main: Suhrkamp Verlag, 1984), pp.795-799.

'On Popular Music' (with George Simpson), *Studies in Philosophy and Social Sciences* 9 (1941), pp.17-48

'Über Jazz', in *Moments Musicaux: neu gedrückte Aufsätze 1928-1962* (Frankfurt: Suhrkamp, 1962), pp.84-125

'Perennial Fashion – Jazz', in *Prisms*, trans. Samuel and Shierry Weber (London: Neville Spearman, 1967), pp.119-132

Philosophy of Modern Music (1949), trans. Anne G. Mitchell and Wesley Blomster (London: Sheed & Ward, 1973). Original: *Philosophie der neuen Musik* (1949), *Gesammelte Schriften* 12 (Frankfurt am Main:

Suhrkamp, 1975). The English translation translates the title inaccurately as 'Philosophy of Modern Music'. Throughout this book the title *Philosophy of New Music* is preferred.

Minima Moralia (1951), transl. E. F. N. Jephcott (London: Verso, 1974)

Introduction to the Sociology of Music (1962), trans. F. B. Ashton (New York: Seabury Press, 1976)

'Music and technique', transl. Wesley Blomster, *Telos*, 32 (1977), pp. 6-88

'On the fetish character in music and the regression of listening', transl. anon., in *The Essential Frankfurt School Reader*, ed. A. Arato and F. Gebhardt (Oxford: Basil Blackwell, 1978), pp.270-99

Aesthetic Theory, ed. Gretel Adorno and Rolf Tiedemann, trans. Christian Lenhardt (London: Routledge and Kegan Paul, 1984), *Ästhetische Theorie*, *Gesammelte Schriften* 7 (Frankfurt am Main: Suhrkamp, 1970; 2nd edn, 1972). Page references in this essay are to the Suhrkamp Taschenbuch Wissenschaft edition (1977)

Negative Dialectics (1966), trans. E. B. Ashton (London: Routledge and Kegan Paul, 1973)

Vorlesungen zur Ästhetik (1967-68) (Zurich: Mayer, 1973)

'Theses on the Sociology of Art' (1967), trans. Brian Trench, *Birmingham Working Papers in Cultural Studies* 2 (1972)

'On the Problem of Musical Analysis', trans. and introduced by Max Paddison, *Music Analysis* 1/2 (July 1982), pp.169-87

'To Describe, Understand and Explain' (with Lucien Goldmann), in Lucien Goldmann, *Cultural Creation in Modern Society*, trans. Bart Grahl (St Louis: Telos, 1976), Appendix 3

The Jargon of Authenticity (1964), trans. Knut Tarnowski and Frederick Will (London: Routledge and Kegan Paul, 1973)

'Ideen zur Musiksoziologie' (1959), in *Klangfiguren: Musikalische Schriften I*, *Gesammelte Schriften* 16 (Frankfurt am Main: Suhrkamp, 1978), pp.9-23

'Commitment', in *The Frankfurt School Reader*, pp.300-18

'Gebrauchsmusik' (1924), *Musikalische Schriften IV*, *Gesammelte Schriften* 19 (Frankfurt am Main: Suhrkamp, 1984), pp.445-7

Dissonanzen: Musik in der verwalteten Welt (Göttingen: Vandenhoek and Rüprecht, 1956; 5th edition, 1972)

'Theses on Art and Religion Today', in *Noten zur Literatur*, *Gesammelte Schriften* 11 (Frankfurt am Main: Suhrkamp, 1974) (original in English), pp.647-53

Der getreue Korrepetitor, *Gesammelte Schriften* 15 (Frankfurt am Main: Suhrkamp, 1976)

Berg: Der Meister des kleinsten Übergangs, Gesammelte Schriften 13 (Frankfurt am Main: Suhrkamp, 1971)

Klangfiguren (1959), in *Gesammelte Schriften* 16 (Frankfurt/Main: Suhrkamp, 1978)

Musikalische Schriften V, *Gesammelte Schriften* 18 (Frankfurt am Main: Suhrkamp, 1984)

'Über das gegenwärtige Verhältnis von Philosophie und Musik' (1953), *Musikalische Schriften V, Gesammelte Schriften*, 18 (Frankfurt am Main: Suhrkamp, 1974), pp.149-78

Versuch über Wagner (1952), *Gesammelte Schriften* 13; trans. Rodney Livingstone as *In Search of Wagner* (London: NLB, 1981)

'Cultural Criticism and Society', in *Prisms*, trans. Samuel and Shierry Weber (London: Neville Spearman, 1967), pp. 17-34

'Of Barricades and Ivory Towers – An Interview with T.W. Adorno' (1968), *Encounter* 33 (September 1969), pp.63-9

'Letters to Walter Benjamin', trans. Harry Zohn, in Ernst Bloch et al., *Aesthetics and Politics*, ed. Ronald Taylor (London: NLB, 1977), pp.110-141

Kompositionen, ed. Heinz-Klaus Metzger and Rainer Riehn (Munich: Edition Text + Kritk, 1980)

2. Works by Writers Associated with the Frankfurt School

Benjamin, Walter, *The Origin of German Tragic Drama*, trans, John Osborne, with an Introduction by George Steiner (London: NLB, 1977)

Benjamin, Walter, *Illuminations*, trans. Harry Zohn, ed. Hannah Arendt (London: Fontana/Collins, 1970)

Bloch, Ernst et al., *Aesthetics and Politics*, ed. Ronald Taylor (London: NLB, 1977)

Bürger, Peter, *Theory of the Avant-Garde* (1964), trans. Michael Shaw (Manchester: Manchester University Press, 1984; original, 1974)

Habermas, Jürgen, 'Modernity – An Incomplete Project', in *Postmodern Culture*, ed. Hal Foster (London: Pluto Press, 1985)

Habermas, Jürgen, 'The Tasks of a Critical Theory of Society', trans. Thomas McCarthy, in *Critical Theory and Society*, eds. Stephen Eric Bonner and Douglas MacKay Kellner (London: Routledge and Kegan Paul, 1989), pp.292-312

Habermas, Jürgen, *The Philosophical Discourse of Modernity* (1985), trans. Frederick Lawrence (Cambridge: Polity Press, 1987)

Horkheimer, Max, 'On the Problem of Truth' (1935), in *The Essential Frankfurt School Reader*, ed. Andrew Arato and Eike Gebhardt (Oxford: Blackwell, 1978), pp.407-43

Horkheimer, Max, (ed.), *Zeugnisse: Theodor W. Adorno zum 60. Geburtstag* (Frankfurt/Main: Europäische Verlagsanstalt, 1963)

Horkheimer, Max, *Traditionelle und kritische Theorie* (Frankfurt/Main: Suhrkamp Verlag, 1970)

Marcuse, Herbert, 'Philosophy and Critical Theory' (1937), trans. Jeremy J. Shapiro, *Critical Theory and Society: A Reader*, ed. Stephen Eric Bronner and Douglas MacKay Kellner (London & New York: Routledge, 1989), pp.58-74

Wellmer, Albrecht, 'Reason, Utopia, and the Dialectic of Enlightenment', in *Habermas and Modernity*, ed. Richard J. Bernstein (Cambridge: Polity Press, 1985, pp.35-66

3. Works on Critical Theory and Adorno Consulted

Agger, Ben, 'On Happiness and the damaged Life', in *On Critical Theory*, ed. John O'Neill (New York and London: Seabury Press/Heinemann, 1976), pp.12-33

Bernstein, Richard J. (ed.), *Habermas and Modernity* (Cambridge: Polity Press, 1985)

Blomster, Wesley, 'Sociology of Music: Adorno and Beyond', *Telos* 28 (1976), pp.81-112

Konrad Boehmer, 'Der Korrepetitor am Werk – Probleme des Materialbegriffs bei Adorno', *Zeitschrift für Musiktheorie* 4 (1973), pp.28-33

Buck-Morss, Susan, *The Origin of Negative Dialectics: Theodor W. Adorno, Walter Benjamin, and the Frankfurt Institute* (London: Harvester, 1977)

Cahn, Michael, 'Subversive Mimesis: Theodor W. Adorno and the Modern Impasse of Critique', in *Mimesis in Contemporary Theory*, Vol. 1, ed. Mihai Spariosu (Philadelphia: Benjamin, 1984)

Dahlhaus, Carl, 'Adornos Begriff des musikalischen Materials', in *Zur Terminologie der Musik des 20. Jahrhunderts: Bericht über das zweite Kolloquium*, ed. H.H. Eggebrecht (Stuttgart, 1974), pp.9-21

de la Motte, Diether, 'Adornos musikalische Analysen', in *Adorno und die Musik*, ed. Otto Kolleritsch (Graz: Universal, 1979), pp.62-53

Etzkorn, K. P., 'Sociologists and Music', in *Music and Society: The Later Writings of Paul Honigsheim*, ed. K. P. Etzkorn (New York: Wiley, 1973), pp.3-40

Gendron, Bernard, 'Theodor Adorno meets the Cadillacs', in T. Modleski (ed.), *Studies in Entertainment: Critical Approaches to Mass Culture* (Bloomington: Indiana, 1986), pp.18-36.

Grenz, Friedemann, 'Zur architektonischen Stellung der Ästhetik in der Philosophie Adornos', in *Theodor W. Adorno: Text + Kritik*, ed. Heinz Ludwig Arnold (Munich: Edition Text + Kritik, 1977)

Geuss, Raymond, *The Idea of a Critical Theory: Habermas & the Frankfurt School* (Cambridge: Cambridge University Press, 1981)

Hullot-Kentor, Bob, 'Adorno's Aesthetic Theory: The Translation', *Telos* 65 (Fall 1985), pp.143-7

Huyssen, Andreas, *After the Great Divide: Modernism, Mass Culture, Postmodernism* (Bloomington: Indiana University Press, 1986)

Jameson, Fredric, *Marxism and Form* (Princeton: Princeton University, 1971)

Jay, Martin, *The Dialectical Imagination: A History of the Frankfurt School and the Institute of Social Research 1923-1950* (London: Heinemann, 1973)

Jay, Martin *Adorno* (London: Fontana/Coilins, 1984).

Jiminez, Marc, *Adorno: art, idéologie et théorie de l'art* (Paris: Union Générale d'Éditions, 1973)

Lenhardt, Christian, 'Reply to Hullot-Kentor', *Telos*, No. 65 (Fall 1985), pp.147-52

Lyotard, Jean-Franois, *The Postmodern Condition: A Report on Knowledge*, trans. Geoff Bennington and Brian Massumi, with a Foreword by Frederic Jameson (Manchester: Manchester University, 1984; orig. French, Editions de Minuit, 1979)

Paddison, Max, 'The Critique Criticised: Adorno and Popular Music', in *Popular Music 2: Theory and Method*, ed. Richard Middleton and David Horn (Cambridge: CUP,1982), pp.201-18

Paddison, Max, 'Adorno's *Aesthetic Theory*', *Music Analysis* 6/3 (October 1987), pp.355-77

Paddison, Max, The Language-character of Music: Some Motifs in Adorno', *Journal of the Royal Musical Association* 116/2 (1991), pp.267-79

Paddison, Max, *Adorno's Aesthetics of Music* (Cambridge: Cambridge University Press, 1993)

Rose, Gillian, *The Melancholy Science: An Introduction to the Thought of Theodor W. Adorno* (London: Macmillan, 1978)

Sandner, Wolfgang, 1973. 'Popularmusik als somatisches Stimulans: Adornos Kritik der "leichten Musik", in *Adorno und die Musik*, ed. Otto Kolleritsch (Graz), pp.123ff

Steuermann, Eduard, 'Briefe an Theodor W. Adorno', in *Zeugnisse: Theodor W. Adorno zum 60. Geburtstag*, ed. Max Horkheimer (Frankfurt/Main: Europäische Verlagsanstalt, 1963)

Subotnik, Rose Rosengard, *Developing Variations: Style and Ideology in Western Music* (Minneapolis & Oxford: University of Minnesota Press, 1991)

Therborn, Göran, 'The Frankfurt School', *New Left Review* 63 (1970), pp.65-96

Weber, Samuel, 'Translating the Untranslatable', in Adorno, *Prisms: Cultural Criticism and Society*, trans. Samuel and Shierry Weber (London: Neville Spearman, 1967), pp.9-15

Wishart, Trevor, 'On Radical Culture', in *Whose Music? A Sociology of Musical Languages*, John Shepherd, Phil Virden, Graham Vuliamy and Trevor Wishart (New Brunswick and London: Transaction Books, 1977), pp.233-56

Wolin, Richard, 'The De-aestheticization of Art: On Adorno's Ästhetische Theorie', *Telos* 41 (Fall 1979), pp.105-27

Zuidervaart, Lambert, 'Refractions: Truth in Adorno's Aesthetic Theory' (Diss., Vrije Universiteit te Amsterdam, 1981).

Zuidervaart, Lambert, 'Adorno, Aesthetic Theory' [review], *The Journal of Aesthetics and Art Theory*, 44/2 (Winter 1985)

Zuidervaart, Lambert, *Adorno's Aesthetic Theory: The Redemption of Illusion* (Cambridge, Mass. & London: The MIT Press, 1991)

4. Other Works Consulted

Biddle, Ian, 'Autonomy, Ontology and the Ideal: Music Theory and Philosophical Aesthetics in Early Nineteenth-Century German Thought' (PhD. Diss., University of Newcastle-upon-Tyne, 1995)

Clarke, David, 'Parting Glances: Aesthetic Solace or Act of Complicity?', *Musical Times* Vol. 134 (December 1993), pp.680-684

Dahlhaus, Carl, *Foundations of Music History* (1967), trans. J.B. Robinson (Cambridge: Cambridge University Press, 1983)

Frith, Simon, *Sound Effects: Youth, leisure, and the politics of rock'n'roll* (London: Constable, 1983)

Hobsbawm, Eric, *The Age of Revolution 1789-1848* (London: Weidenfeld & Nlcolson, 1962; Sphere/Cardinal, 1988)

Kater, Michael H., *Different Drummers: Jazz in the Culture of Nazi Germany* (New York & Oxford: Oxford University Press, 1992)

Marx, Karl *Capital*, Vol. 1 (1867), trans. Ben Fowkes (Harmondsworth: Penguin, 1976)

McFarlane, James, 'The Mind of Modernism', in Malcolm Bradbury and James McFarlane (eds.), *Modernism 1890-1930* (Harmondsworth: Penguin, 1976, 1986), pp.71-93

McClary, Susan, *Feminine Endings: Music, Gender and Sexuality* (Minnesota & Oxford: University of Minnesota Press, 1991)

Middleton, Richard, *Studying Popular Music* (Milton Keynes: Open University Press. 1990)

Nestrovski, Arthur, 'Music Theory, Saussure, *Theoria*', *In Theory Only* 10/6 (May 1988)

Runciman, W. G. (ed.), *Weber: Selections in Translation*, trans. Eric Matthews (Cambridge: CUP, 1978)

Said, Edward, *Musical Elaborations* (1991) (London: Vintage Books, 1992)

Shepherd, John, 'The 'Meaning' of Music', in *Whose Music? A Sociology of Musical Languages*, John Shepherd, Phil Virden, Graham Vulliamy and Trevor Wishart (New Brunswick and London: Transaction Books, 1977), pp.53-68

Stuckenschmidt, H.H., *Schoenberg: His Life, World and Work*, trans. Humphrey Searle (London: Calder, 1977)

Vogt, Hans, *Neue Musik seit 1945* (Stuttgart: Reclam, 1962)

Watson, Ben, *Frank Zappa: The Negative Dialectics of Poodle Play* (London: Quartet Books, 1994)

Weber, Max, *The Protestant Ethic and the Spirit of Capitalism* (1904-5), trans. Talcott Parsons (London: George Allen & Unwin, 1930)

Weber, Max, *The Rational and Social Foundations of Music* (1911, 1921), trans. and ed. Don Martindale, Johannes Riedel and Gertrude Neuwirth (Carbondale: Southern Illinois University Press, 1958)

Williams, Alastair, 'New Music and the Claims of Modernity' (PhD diss., University of Oxford, 1991)

Index of Names

Subject Index